THOU HOLDEST
MY RIGHT HAND

THOU HOLDEST MY RIGHT HAND

On Pastoral Care of the Dying

by

D. LOS

Translated by **Theodore Plantinga**

Pastoral Perspectives II

INHERITANCE PUBLICATIONS
NEERLANDIA, ALBERTA, CANADA
PELLA, IOWA, U.S.A.

Canadian Cataloguing in Publication Data

Los, D.
  Thou holdest my right hand

  (Pastoral perspectives ; 2)
  Translation of: Gij hebt mijn rechterhand gevat
  ISBN 0-921100-45-0
  1. Terminally ill—Pastoral counselling of.
I. Title. II. Series.
BV4338.L6813 1993   259'.4   C93-091926-2

Library of Congress Cataloging-in-Publication Data

Los, D., 1917-
  [Gij hebt mijn rechterhand gevat. English]
  Thou holdest my right hand : on pastoral care of the dying / by D. Los ;
translated by Theodore Plantinga.
    p.   cm. — (Pastoral Perspectives ; 2)
  ISBN 0-921100-45-0 (pbk.) : $8.90
  1. Church work with the terminally ill. 2. Death—Religious aspects—Reformed
Church. 1. Title. II. Series.
  BV4338.L6713 1993
  259'.4—dc20   93-39279
                                                                        CIP

Translated by Theodore Plantinga
Cover Picture by Dick M. Barendregt

Originally published as *Gij hebt mijn rechterhand gevat*, (1988)
by Oosterbaan & Le Cointre, Goes, the Netherlands
Published with permission.

Published simultaneously in U.S.A. by Inheritance Publications
P.O. Box 366, Pella, Iowa 50219 Tel. & Fax (515) 628-3804

ISBN 0-921100-45-0

Printed in Canada by
Premier Printing Ltd. Winnipeg, MB

Contents

Chapter 1

By Way of Introduction

"Be of sober spirit, be on the alert." (I Pet. 5:8)

A sober approach

When two or more people write on the same topic, they usually come up with different results. This should not surprise us; it is not strange, nor is it a reason for concern. Instead we should admit simply that people are not all alike. The way we talk and think is bound up to some extent with our nature. There is variation within God's creation.

We ought to be thankful for the variation that exists; indeed, we should consider ourselves as blessed. If it were not for created differences, it would be a rather tiresome business in the world — and also in the church. We would soon get tired of looking at each other, and of talking together and writing to one another.

The pluriformity within the human race, including the body of believers, provides an element of excitement in our relations with one another. It makes it possible for us to have exciting conversations, and for us to develop in various ways. It adds interest and vivacity to human relationships and makes social life colorful.

This is why recitals or descriptions of facts and events by different people often vary — sometimes to the point that we are struck by the differences. You come across this sort of thing in everyday experience as you read articles in books, newspapers, and magazines. You also find this out when you listen to lectures and speeches at meetings or to programs on the radio. What differences there are in the way people express themselves and approach a subject and work it out!

And so we see daily that one person differs from another. This is not something that distresses us — in fact, we do not make a problem of it at all. Even though we all have our preferences, the differences we see need not lead to conflict. We simply do not make an issue of such differences. Nor do we suggest that those who are different from the rest of us should be imprisoned.

No, we feel no need whatsoever to make an issue of the differences that exist. For we remember the Bible's appeal to be *sober*. And if we are sober, we have a sense of reality — which is not something we possess of ourselves. It is actually a gift of God.

And so we are willing to shake hands with one another in a posture of understanding and agreement. This also applies to you and me — that's how things are.

Let's be on the alert too

If you have a good sense of what's real, you have reason to be thankful. How would we ever get along in our social life without a sense of reality? You know what they say about people — including church people: "There are as many opinions as there are people." Without a sense of reality, we would have a hard time of it indeed.

This much seems clear to me. But there is more to be said. The differences between people do not result solely from God's pluriform creation. Some of them are rooted in the fall into sin. This truth should also be obvious to us, and it should make us feel uneasy.

It is quite something when you pause and reflect. Ever since Adam, our first father, turned his back on God, the antithesis has cut right through our race (Gen. 3:15). For ages, believers and unbelievers have stood diametrically opposed to one another. The opposition between the truth and the lie, an opposition which is never to be reconciled, still stands. And it may not be denied or downplayed for even a moment.

Therefore the apostle instructs us to be both sober and on the alert — and never to separate these two qualities (I Pet. 5:8). What the apostle says here is not a piece of advice which we are free to accept or reject; rather, it is a command that is in effect for us today. It applies to everyone who fears the Lord and takes His Word seriously: keep a cool head, and keep your eyes and ears wide open. The LORD, our Covenant God, is by no means indifferent to what we say or write, or how we read or listen. Rather, He wants us to uphold the one just norm in everything we do. That norm is His trustworthy Word, which stands firm and must be accepted without any reservation.

Working under the norm

I hope it is already clear to you from what I have written that it is not up to *us* to determine what is pleasing to the Lord and beneficial for our fellow human beings. All such things are determined by God!

I believe it is necessary to emphasize this point at the outset. The reader has the right to expect a clearly articulated position and a positive orientation. This applies not just to the conclusions we may reach but also to the way in which the topic is taken up.

In recent years there have been many books and articles published that are intended to give some "guidance" at the time of death. I do not wish to create the impression that all of this material is of the same sort, for such a conclusion would not be fair. Moreover, I should not generalize. Yet I must say something about what I have discovered — to my disappointment — in my reading of these writings. So much of what I have read breathes the spirit that is typical of our time — horizontalism. In some of the writings this attitude is like a heavy film on top of the text.

While I was reading books and articles of this sort, I often wondered how so many pastors and others who are charged with helping the sick and dying imagine that they can approach people in the last phase of their earthly life with such cheap and superficial talk. I would not know what to do with myself if I had been busy counseling the terminally ill in such a fashion. I would feel guilty before God and man. All that horizontalistic talk — however well intended and neatly expressed — has almost nothing to do with "pastoral help," as far as I can tell.

No effort to be of help which does not allow *Scripture* to have the first and last word can be pleasing to God. Nor can such "help" be profitable to our neighbor who receives it in the sense that it enables him to taste something of the mercy of God in Jesus Christ. And isn't the mercy of God what we are aiming to bring across when we offer pastoral help? Didn't the Savior say in Luke 6:36, "Be merciful, just as your Father is merciful?"

If we want to understand something of God's mercy, then, and if we propose to pass it along to others, we must be sure we are working under the norm.

Pastoral help

My purpose in writing this book is to offer some guidance to those who give pastoral care to people who are dying. When you hear the word "pastoral," you may well be inclined to think it refers to the work of a minister. He is the one who, first and foremost, does the work of a shepherd in the congregation he serves, and also in the hospital, and perhaps in the nursing home if he is a chaplain.

Naturally, I do not wish to deny these things. But it is a mistake to limit the term "pastoral" to this kind of work. The sort of help I am talking about must be understood in a much broader sense — it is part of the calling of *every* believer.

A believer, as a member of Christ, shares in His anointing. The Holy Spirit has given him gifts. And he has been renewed in God's image. All of this equips him to fulfil the threefold office of prophet, priest and king (see Q. & A. 32 of the Heidelberg Catechism).

Because of this threefold office, a Christian is obliged to serve God and his neighbor in a loving way all down the line. In this regard we *all* possess a pastoral calling. We must throw ourselves completely into the challenge of being of service to people who need help. And then I think first of all of people who are dying.

*   *   *   *   *

The word "pastoral" is rooted in "pastor," which means shepherd. We think of Psalm 23, which the Holy Spirit uses to teach us who and what the Lord is for us.

Because He is our Shepherd, we lack nothing. The good Shepherd sees to it that we can be calm when we are in need or in difficult circumstances. Even in the face of death, we need not be afraid. There is one thing that must stand firm for us: the LORD is with us! Not for a moment does He lose sight of us. He does not let go of us or abandon us (see Heb. 13:5–6).

This reality does not only apply to you as an individual but also to others who believe as you do. And so we can look to Psalm 23 to set the course we must follow when we offer *pastoral* help.

We are eager to have others share in the things we may know and experience in faith. It is also our wish for others that they will experience God's pastoral concern for them. But how is this concern to be manifested in their lives? The answer is that *we ourselves* are to be active in this regard! We do so in the knowledge that the Good Shepherd wishes to use us as His fellow workers.

It is in this light, I believe, that our priestly calling becomes real in the midst of our lives today. It is our privilege to let something of God's mercy in Jesus Christ stream forth from us. We know that we are obliged to make this divine mercy flow from us to our neighbors and to all that are right around us. We want to show that mercy to the chronically ill, to the mentally handicapped, and to people who are on their deathbed.

When we find within ourselves the desire to be of service in this way, we realize the high value and absolute indispensability of the Church — yes, indeed, the *Church!* After all, the Church is the gathering of believers. We confess that it is the work community of the Holy Spirit (see Q. & A. 55 of the Heidelberg Catechism).

Because we as believers, both individually and corporately, have communion with the Lord Christ and share in His gifts and treasures, every one of us is obliged to apply those gifts for the use and welfare of the other members. Moreover, we must do so willingly and joyfully. When we hold God's Word in our hands we see that extending "pastoral help" is the calling of each one of us. We may not shove off such care on other people or leave it to be done solely by the minister or the elders.

It ought to be fixed and established for us that the kind of help we are talking about has nothing to do with the notion of some activity we may take up or drop as *we* see fit; rather, it is an obligation that flows from our *priestly* task as Christians. As believers we are to take this work very seriously.

*   *   *   *   *

What place is there in all of this for the pastor as "the undershepherd of Christ?" His task is to stimulate and promote the Christian calling in the community in a "professional manner." In the carrying out of his special office, he must take the lead and set an example. In part because of his own experience and his practice, he is in a position to mobilize the congregation's "support troops," instructing and activating them in the name of the Great Shepherd.

In this way a work community comes into existence, and it, in turn, will be important in rendering support to those who, in the last phase of their life, cannot manage on their own. Through some practical examples, I will try to show you how much joy there is in carrying out this task.

Terminal patients

We use the term "terminal" to refer to people who are very seriously ill, people who, according to the doctor, will die within a foreseeable period of time. Such patients are engaged in the process of dying. Thus we may think of them as living on the border between life and death. Many such sick people spend their last days in a nursing care facility.

In recent years we have heard many voices suggesting that the terminally ill should be cared for *at home* if at all possible — or at least in a more intimate family-like setting. I will come back to this matter later.

It seems to me that we should support such efforts and emphases. It is certainly understandable for people who are dying to say that they wish to spend their final days in a familiar and trusted environment.

And if this is not possible in certain cases, we must do our best to optimize the circumstances in the hospital or the nursing facility. There are some things that can be done in this direction. My own experience in providing spiritual care has shown me how worthwhile such efforts are. The condition that makes it possible is a willingness on the part of various professionals to work together in a spirit of agreement. The people I am thinking of here include, among others, those who offer medical, nursing, social, and spiritual assistance — doctors, nurses, family members, and the pastor.

Even though the members of each of these groups have their separate tasks, they will function most effectively if their aim is not to work on their own. Instead they should try to work closely together as a team with members of the other groups. The encouragement, advice, and exchange of ideas will help to guarantee the best possible level of care.

It has been demonstrated that this ideal in terms of care of the terminally ill can best be attained when the various participants have the same religious convictions and are one in the Spirit.

A meaningful title

In the light of what I have written so far, the title I have chosen for this book will surely seem apt. The words "Thou hast taken hold of my right hand" occur in Psalm 73:23. In using these words as my title, I do not mean to pluck them from the context in which they occur in the Bible.

It appears that Asaph, the writer of this psalm, was a brother to whom nothing human was foreign. One reason why this passage speaks to us so eloquently is because it is as though he takes the words right out of our own mouth.

At first he seemed to run completely stuck in his vision and judgment of human life. He had a very hard time accepting the fact that unbelievers often appear to fare better than believers.

Indeed, he admitted that God is good to Israel (vs. 1). But it was a riddle to him why God directs affairs in this world in such a manner that His children seem in many respects to be worse off than those who refuse to serve the LORD. He could not make sense of it. He wrestled with this question, for to him it was an offense, a thorn in the flesh, a torment for his spirit (see vs. 13–16).

But he did not remain stuck there forever. On the very point that was unacceptable for him, the LORD allowed Asaph to attain clarity. How did this clarity come about? In the temple — through the Word of truth. It was there that he caught sight of the reality of God. What is really going on here on earth?

By simply increasing their possessions in a manner that shows no concern, the godless are actually moving along a path of deadly danger. Unless they are converted, their end is darkness and destruction. In the coming divine judgment, it will be their lot to be despised (vs. 20).

What is it, on the other hand, that gives us true joy and certainty? Being near to God — being in covenant fellowship with Him continually. Who made such fellowship possible? The LORD did so Himself in His free good pleasure toward us. Asaph confessed, "Thou holdest my right hand." This is a confession with far-reaching significance.

It is not the case that *we* go to God in order to make covenant with Him. The LORD, in His gracious love, comes to us. Even before we realized what was happening, *He* made us His children and established fellowship with us. This fact is signified and sealed in our baptism.

On that basis we must confess and experience that *all* our strength (pay special attention to the term "right hand") comes from God alone. This applies to the days when we are hale and hearty, but it is also true of those who are ill or handicapped. And it remains true when we lie on our deathbed!

*   *   *   *   *

"Thou holdest my right hand!" This is a very meaningful title for a book. Through what follows in these pages, I hope you will come to see that this certainty means that when an appeal is made to you to extend pastoral care, your effort will not be in vain.

Not only is the person needing help of infinite value, but your help is also indispensable — for Christ's sake it must not be withheld. Consider the following by way of illustration.

From jealousy to thankfulness

There's no such thing as chance: nothing happens by accident. Everything is ordered by God in accordance with the counsel of His will (see Eph. 1:11). I believe this, but it has never made me passive — quite the contrary. Instead it has intensified my experience of what *God*, according to my conviction, has placed on my path.

What I am thinking of especially is the obligation to be of assistance to a seriously ill woman in whose life there had been a remarkable reversal. That reversal made it possible for me to offer her pastoral care right up to her death.

Making the first contact with her was simple. She was lying in a hospital room which I visited regularly because a member of my congregation was there, from whom I learned that the woman in question would also appreciate being visited. I had already noticed that this "neighbor" listened attentively when I read the Scriptures with the woman from my congregation.

I took advantage of the opportunity to speak with this "neighbor" about the passage I was reading. She was receptive and was happy to talk with me. Because she was "terminal," she was scheduled to be moved in a week to a nursing facility, where she would remain for the time left to her.

She made an urgent appeal to me to visit her while she was there. My reaction was: I will do so gladly!

Her upbringing had not taught her anything about God or the Bible. And what you don't know about doesn't concern you either. But her attitude had changed after she spent many months in the hospital, where she underwent all sorts of diagnostic procedures. The outcome was that her illness could not be healed medically: the specialist gave her only a few more months to live.

At first this news shocked her deeply. Much of the time she didn't know where to turn, for she loved being alive and had drunk deeply of the well of life. And she had never thought about death. Why concern oneself with such a thing? After all, when you die it's all over — right? Therefore, enjoy life, for there's no tomorrow.

The situation in which she now found herself was so sad because she had to go through her anguish all alone. Rarely did friends come to visit. Her parents ignored her. They had gotten a divorce some years before and took no interest in her situation after that.

In that tragic set of circumstances she was struck by the fact that the woman in the next bed (the one who belonged to my congregation) could be so calm and joyful. And she got a lot of visitors. Even her minister came regularly. Moreover, this woman read the Bible every day, and she prayed.

The woman left all alone noted all these things, and at a certain point she even became *jealous* of her believing neighbor. She eventually confessed these things to me honestly. And that's why she was so *thankful* for finally coming into contact with the Gospel.

Her gratitude grew deeper in the months that followed. The LORD permitted me to extend pastoral care to her for another six months. We used that time to the full. Sometimes I visited her several times per week. As long as she was able to talk, we discussed the heart of the Gospel. You would have to have been there to know what it was like — never have I had a more grateful "student." She drank in the instruction I offered her, wanting to know more and more. Spiritually she blossomed!

While this was going on, she was also visited on occasion by members of my congregation. It was obvious how much she enjoyed those visits. Naturally, "faith" was discussed during those visits — she couldn't leave the subject alone.

Things finally developed to the point that she confessed, to her great joy, that she had found in her Lord and Savior something for which she had yearned for years, yet without realizing it. How thankful she was to know with certainty that she, too, could lay claim to Christ's sacrifice for the forgiveness of sins and real, life-preserving salvation!

Together we thanked our faithful covenant God for her salvation. As she lay dying, I held her right hand. That made her feel secure.

I said to her, "This is how the LORD holds your right hand. He has directed your life in accordance with His counsel. And now He is taking you to glory." She could say nothing more by this point. But I will never forget the thankful look in her eyes.

* * * * *

It is good to be near to God. It is indispensable to have the Lord of hosts as our refuge. We will never finish telling about all His works. And even though we repeatedly have to start all over in the task of telling about Him, we do not allow ourselves to become guilty of propagating cheap stories of salvation. We want nothing to do with such stories. For the salvation which our God has in mind for sinful people, people who in themselves are lost, is *free* — but it's not *cheap!*

Chapter 2

The Biblical View of Life and Death

". . . and man became a living being."   (Gen. 2:7)

"I will give thanks to Thee, for I am fearfully and wonderfully made."   (Ps. 139:14)

". . . and so death spread to all men, because all sinned . . ."   (Rom. 5:12)

The current spirit of the age

People are not soon finished when they talk about life here on earth. Much has been written about this matter over the years, in all kinds of variations and spirits, both positive and negative. How a person writes depends on how he regards human life and on the starting point he uses. Naturally, we must take into account the experiences that have shaped a person's thinking and attitudes regarding life.

The "vision" of life which people have today is ever more horizontalistic. The kind of thinking which God teaches us through His Word is increasingly giving way to thinking that does not rise above the surface of the earth, the kind of thinking that allows man to imagine that *he* is sovereign. And this limitation on human thinking brings certain consequences with it.

Anyone who walks through life wearing blinkers thereby limits his field of vision. This seems crystal-clear to me. Anyone who cannot look beyond the end of his nose will not have a very high estimate of the value of life. In his thinking and actions, he will not get below the surfaces. Because his horizon does not extend much beyond what is immediately before him, he lacks the kind of perspective that can have a liberating effect. Life, for him, becomes an adventure with constantly shifting stages. It may seem stirring and exciting, but it becomes

18

unbelievably dull and tiresome. And in any case, all that such a person desires and strives for is played out within the comparatively small space between the cradle and the grave.

When you live in this way, you do not always attain what you want. There are so many factors at work which are not under your control. People say that "fate," in particular, has a lot to say about our lives. If "fate" is against you, you had better step aside, for it cannot be defeated or resisted or overthrown.

Yes, and then there is also that incalculable moment when you encounter *death*. It makes its appearance sooner or later, and then it's all over with you. Your file is closed. At that point life is of no more benefit to you. What was it that you lived and worked for all those years?

When you take a careful look, you realize that all your toil and trouble was largely in vain. Where did it get you? What do you have to show for it? If you enjoy any fruits of your labors, they will not last long. And the enjoyment is made bitter by the shadow of death falling across your path. Do you dare deny it?

And do you know what many people find very hard to swallow? The thought that life will continue in its normal course *after* they have died. The people at work will manage to get along without them. Family and friends will get over the feeling of loss and will again take part in the normal process of living.

What a painful thought! Doesn't it prove that you as a person are not quite as important and indispensable as you like to think or suggest? And isn't this realization a slap in the face? It leads us to wonder why we as human beings allow ourselves to get so wound up. What sense does it make to exert yourself so heavily that eventually you get a heart attack or a stroke?

If you'll just take it a little easier, you won't be such a good candidate for a breakdown. After all, it's up to you. Forewarned is forearmed. Well then . . . .

We must all admit that the sketch above is not a caricature. Every day you encounter such a mentality among people you meet. It often happens that life does not give people what they are hoping for. And because death lurks in the background to break the spell unexpectedly, there's not much point in starting anything. Well, then, what are we to do?

And don't try to tell me that this mentality does not affect *you*. Instead you should admit that we must make a special effort to plant our spiritual feet firmly on the ground if we are to avoid being infected by such thinking. It gets going in our heads all too easily. Many have drowned in such a sea of despair even before they realized they were in the water.

Don't forget how deeply the spirit of the present age has eaten into the way we think about life. Indifference and pessimism, those bitter fruits of the current secular outlook on life, have shown how disadvantageous they are for anyone who tries to come to a proper understanding of human existence. For example, they have a disastrous effect on our estimation of our place in relation to the process of work. As a Christian you stand there amazed at what you see!

Perhaps you are wondering what all of this has to do with our topic. The answer is that when you are offering pastoral care to the dying, you encounter these very questions. You may well find yourself facing a certain indifference in the face of life and death, an indifference which has not been worked through on an emotional level and which can explode in the face of the person offering pastoral care. How impotent and helpless one can feel in such a situation! Let me give you an example from actual practice.

A sharp contrast

One day I was visiting a young man who had fallen ill. He had a deep desire to survive, for he had many plans he had not yet carried out. Not long before, he had become engaged to be married, and now he wanted to finish his studies as quickly as possible. Then he would find a job and get married.

He and his fiancée were very grateful to the LORD for the fact that they had found one another. They were nicely suited to each other, for they were one in faith and love and thus could talk very well together. For them it seemed a special pleasure that they stood on the same basis, that they possessed the same Word, and that both were straightforwardly Reformed in profession. But now this illness!

The young man confessed to me that he had a very hard time accepting what was happening to him. He could not understand why the blessings that had flowered in his life now seemed to wither away so suddenly. More than once I found him very dejected, in a pit of despair — to the point that he grew rebellious. In such a situation he could not pray, for he did not want to be a hypocrite before the LORD.

It was a good thing that he and his fiancée understood each other so well on this point. They took turns encouraging each other in a Christian manner. And the things they said to each other did some good, even though the need for such encouragement came up time and again.

I tried to contribute to the discussion by pointing out that our faithful covenant God assesses our ups and downs as to their value. He does this much more wisely than we ourselves or our fellow human beings could ever do. It is for this reason that He leads us to experience just how great His loving mercy is in relation to human weaknesses and shortcomings. Instead of rejecting us, He draws us closer to Himself. He knows how much we need Him.

It was a fine and open discussion we had. I, too, was encouraged by it. We were able to agree on how we should end our time together through prayer and the reading of a certain passage of Scripture.

As is my custom, I asked the other patients in the room whether it would be all right if I also prayed aloud for them. One of the patients was absolutely opposed to my suggestion. He was a very elderly man — over eighty, I judged — and he told me that he wanted nothing to do with "all that nonsense." Naturally, I did not press him on this matter. But after completing my visit with the young man, I felt I should talk with the old man for a few minutes.

He then proceeded to tell me a thing or two. Even though he was weak and emaciated, he directed an emotional tirade at me. He let me know in no uncertain terms that he wanted nothing to do with any effort to "pull the wool over people's eyes." No one had ever been able to prove God's existence to him. He said that since he was suffering from a horrible cancer of the lungs, he would rather be dead today than tomorrow, for then he would be free of all pain and misery.

It remained a monologue: he did all the talking. Because he got more and more excited, he fell into such a fit of coughing that it looked as though he might choke to death. To keep him from getting any more worked up, I took leave of him with just a few words, and with a heavy heart. How powerless I felt at that moment — and how dissatisfied!

*   *   *   *   *

I had a hard time shaking that experience off. What a contrast between two terminal patients in the same room!

A week later, when I visited the young man in the hospital again, I found out that the old man with whom I had spoken had died a few days before. Right up to the time of his death, he had continued to make fun of ministers and their "pious chatter."

However, the young brother I was visiting told me that what had happened during my previous visit had enabled him to make some progress. He found he was able to thank the LORD for the privilege of possessing "the right view of life and death" through His Word. We talked about this matter for some time. And as we talked, we felt the wealth that comes from the firm assurance of *knowing* that we are Christ's — in life and in death — which is our only comfort.

Our life is exclusively God's work

Every human being owes his origin and existence exclusively to God. This we learn from the Bible.

In Genesis 2 we read how the LORD God formed man from the dust of the earth and breathed the breath of life into his nostrils. That was how man became a living being (vs. 7).

The LORD also wanted to provide for the continuation of Adam's line. With His own hand, therefore, He gave to Adam the woman who was suited to be with him. The LORD God built the rib which He had taken out of Adam into a woman and brought her to the man (vs. 22).

This first married couple received from God the commission to be fruitful and become numerous. Through sexual intercourse within marriage, their family circle would be expanded. And that's how it must always be: just read Genesis 2:24, and then go on to Matthew 19:5, Mark 10:7, and Ephesians 5:31.

What is emphasized in these passages is that at a certain point in time, the young man leaves the home of his parents. From then on he lives legally and publicly with his wife in the bonds of matrimony. What does the Bible teach us about this matter? It leaves no room for sexual intercourse *before* marriage or for any form of "living together." There is no escaping this conclusion.

It pleases the LORD to have children brought into this world through the route He has designated for us. He forms *human beings* from the very moment of conception. This is another point about which Scripture does not leave us uncertain. Consider the following passage.

In the verses 13–16 of Psalm 139, David confesses that the LORD knew and formed him right from the beginning (conception). The LORD formed his inward parts and knit him together when he was in his mother's womb. David could not stop praising his God because of the fact that his life had been so wonderfully prepared. In faith he was well aware that his frame was not hidden from the LORD when he was being made in secret. The eyes of his God and Savior truly beheld his formless being.

What we read in Job 10 is just as clear. In verse 8 Job declares that God's hand formed and fashioned him completely. In fine poetic form he then proceeds, in verses 10 and 11, to talk about what went on in his mother's womb when he was being formed. He compares the act of conception with the pouring out of milk and the curdling of cheese. With regard to his Maker and Former he writes: "Didst Thou not pour me out like milk, and curdle me like cheese; clothe me with skin and flesh, and knit me together with bones and sinews?"

When the Word of the LORD called Jeremiah, he heard the following: "Before I formed you in the womb I knew you, and before you were born I consecrated you" (Jer. 1:5).

Thus it cannot be denied that our life, from the very beginning, is *God's* work. This fact gives human life great value and never allows it to become completely meaningless. Therefore we must be very careful with our own life and the lives of others. It is not for us to take the power of life and death into our hands.

Human life must not be understood in "biological" terms only. There is more to be said. Using the light provided by the Scriptures, our image of man must be complete.

Our life is spiritual and eternal

In virtue of his creation, man is a rational being possessing understanding, will, and feeling. He also has the capacity to give expression to his thoughts and feelings in words: he can speak and communicate with others.

Adam, the first man, could rightly be called the "crown jewel of creation." He was far above all other creatures and was even elevated above the angels. He was made in God's image, in His likeness (Gen. 1:26).

Just what this means can also be learned from Ephesians 4:24. There we read that the human being delivered by Christ must strive to again become the image of God: "put on the new self, which in the likeness of God has been created in righteousness and holiness of the truth."

As the one who bears God's image, man must serve Him. He has received a task from God. Because of the threefold functioning of that one task (prophet, priest and king), he has received the requisite gifts, i.e. wisdom, righteousness and holiness (see Answer 32 of the Heidelberg Catechism).

It can be said of magnificent man in particular that there was a special bond between him and his Creator — the bond of the Covenant.

This relationship was initiated by God alone, but it was two-sided in its operation.

In that relationship Adam was privileged to serve his God in a unique way. And he was *fully equipped* to do so; there was nothing standing in his way. He knew the LORD and recognized Him and gave himself completely to Him and was permitted to rule with Him over all the creatures. There were three aspects to the task he was to carry out. Adam could rest assured that the way of obedient service in office to God his Creator would lead to a life of eternal glory, praising God (see Answer 6 of the Heidelberg Catechism).

When we bear all of this in mind, we understand that the natural life of man was not something apart, something complete in itself. It was at the same time spiritually determined, and it possessed eternal value. It was a life with three aspects, which could be distinguished but never separated from one another.

Our fall into sin, with all of its consequences, had some devastating effects on this reality. We experience those effects in this life. We see them in the lives of other people — a stream of sickness, handicaps, confinement to bed, suffering, poverty, sorrow. These things are everyday realities. And then, let's not forget that *death* comes to all men.

The Biblical conception of death

Ask a number of people what they think about life and death. You will note that there are many different views. What people think depends on various factors, including their age, their religious allegiance, their basic outlook on life, and the experiences they have had.

It cannot be denied that the way we work through the death of someone we have known has a great deal to do with the way we look ahead to the prospect of *our own death*. After World War II there were some changes to be noted in the way people in the Netherlands thought about this matter, just as there were many other changes that resulted from the war.

When I think back to my own youth, I recall that for many people, death was something mysterious. It filled us with respect. But people didn't talk about it enough. You would hear someone say, "The minister is passing by" (which meant that he was on his way to inform some people that a member of their family had passed away), and that was enough.

More recently, the taboo concerning the mention of death has largely fallen away. There is much more written about death and dying now than there was in former years: these notions have become "common property."

What are the reasons for this change? To begin with, you must not forget that today's world, with its many advances in technology, is much more "open" than the world of our fathers. We see things today that we didn't used to see, and the world has become smaller, as it were. Through newspapers, magazines and television, we are drawn much closer to horrible things that go on in faraway places, which may have frightful consequences in terms of large-scale killings.

In part for these reasons, human beings have grown somewhat accustomed to certain things, and our sensitivity has been dulled. You see this among older people, but even more among the young. A child can stand there with a plastic gun in his hand and say, "Stay right where you are, or I'll shoot you dead!"

You should also bear in mind that the decreasing respect for the Bible in our time cannot help but cloud our understanding of life and death. The decline of the Bible's influence over us plays a very powerful role in our limited, private view of these matters. That's why it is so necessary to look carefully at what *the Scriptures* actually teach us about life and death.

Our starting point must be that God has destined us for *life* — and not for *death*. Death is not something that comes from God; it is a consequence of our willful fall into sin.

Life and death are not the same thing. Neither are they to be placed on the same level or regarded as together forming a unity. Death is the *enemy* of life — a formidable foe whom we must not try to laugh off. We must make no attempt to reconcile life and death with one another.

Death is the consequence of our fall into sin. In Genesis 2:15–17 we read that the LORD God Himself gave man the garden of Eden as a place to live and work. He was supposed to cultivate and protect it.

At the same time man was given permission to eat from the fruit of any tree in the garden — except for "the tree of the knowledge of good and evil." A command was given with regard to that tree, and a stipulation was attached to the command: "In the day that you eat of it you shall surely die."

Thus Adam and his wife knew exactly where they stood. They knew just what would happen if they transgressed the "test command." This is evident from the fact that when Eve was addressed by the devil, who put a false suggestion before her, she responded by repeating correctly what the LORD had said (Gen. 3:2–3).

The threat of punishment ("you shall surely die") was thus heard for the first time in Paradise! This possibility was inseparably connected with the transgression of the command that had been given by God. Before that time the LORD had said nothing about life and death.

We must conclude that when it comes to these two realities, we are dealing with two very serious and consequential results of the fall into sin. In connection with this matter the apostle Paul writes: "Therefore, just as through one man sin entered into the world, and death through sin . . . so death spread to all men, because all sinned" (Rom. 5:12).

Now notice something remarkable. The Bible speaks of human life in three senses: natural, spiritual and eternal. It also speaks of death in these three senses. When man fell into sin in the garden of Eden, death entered the world. After their transgression, Adam and Eve did not directly fall down "lifeless" (in the biological sense) at God's feet. Yet they were immediately banned from paradisal fellowship with God. Since that time, all human beings are "dead" in their "trespasses and sins" (Paul's words in Eph. 2:1). Paul also uses the words "dead in our/ your transgressions" (vs. 5; Col. 2:13).

Because man becomes hardened in his unbelief, this spiritual death eventuates in "eternal death" — the ultimate corruption in hell, which is also called the "second death" (Rev. 2:11; 20:6; 21:8). We must not try to downplay or deny the horrible character of this (second) death, for it is and remains "the last enemy" (I Cor. 15:26). It is never "our friend."

Only through Christ's suffering, death and resurrection is the *element of punishment* taken away for those who believe. Because of what He has done, we can confess with the apostle Paul that our triumph over sin and death and hell is given through our Lord Jesus Christ (I Cor. 15:56).

In the case of all who belong to Christ and are reconciled to God, it can be said that there is *harmony* between life and death. This will be our theme in the next chapter.

Chapter 3

Harmony Between Life and Death

> *". . . he who believes in Me shall live even if he dies, and everyone who lives and believes in Me shall never die."* (John 11:25–26)

> *"For to me, to live is Christ, and to die is gain."* (Phil. 1:21)

> *"For if we died with Him, we shall also live with Him."* (II Tim. 2:11)

The rider on the pale horse

Death is the enemy of life! This will remain so until the end of time. Death is the last enemy and will not be destroyed until Christ returns. Then death will be dethroned once and for all (I Cor. 15:26) and will be swallowed up in victory (vs. 54).

But until things reach that point, it appears that death will have free rein. Every day death attacks and claims thousands of victims. There are people who die at a very advanced age. There are also people who die while they are in the prime of life or are taken away at a very young age. There are many who die of some serious illness or other — diseases of the heart or circulatory system, AIDS, cancer. Many are called away suddenly and unexpectedly through an accident.

Indeed, we are confronted daily with the reality of which Revelation 6:7–8 speaks. After the opening of the fourth seal, the apostle John saw "Death" in person, seated on a pale (ashen) horse. Following him was Hades.

The consequences were disturbing. A fourth of the earth became a mass cemetery. The pain and suffering that flowed from these events are too vast to behold — to say nothing of comprehension. Yes, and then you must go on to read how the rider on that pale horse, that grim enemy, reaches his goal. He does not only use wars, famines and contagious diseases, but also the wild beasts of the earth. It seems to me that the microscopically small organisms that cause all sorts of stubborn and painful ailments and spread them around could be included under this heading.

How relevant to our age! Today we still encounter ailments that puzzle the medical world and can hardly be treated and checked. Poisonous bacteria and highly infectious viruses keep working in quiet, unseen ways; they often claim more victims than wars and traffic accidents.

And then we should remember that when we fight against one kind of bacterium or virus, we may wind up — unwittingly — spreading another one around. Think of the fatal side-effects of certain medicines, sprays, sleeping pills, stimulants, and tranquilizers.

What is the greatest tragedy of our time? That when we seem to be getting somewhere in one area, we are at the same time losing ground in another. Let me give you a striking example. Modern medical science seems to be able to accomplish just about anything — especially when it comes to helping people who are suffering. Amazing operations are performed, and surprising organ transplants now seem possible. Death can be warded off and life prolonged. But in the meantime . . . ?

In the meantime the number of dead is even greater than before — and it happens by way of the very same medical science! Think of the legalized murder of children (abortion) and the attempts to legitimize the killing of old people under the label of "euthanasia." Here you have some completely typical and yet notorious examples of the inner dividedness of man in the end time — man who mistakenly thinks himself to be sovereign.

And yet, it appears that the last enemy also has the last word. Is there anyone in a position to block the advance of the rider on the pale horse? No person or method, no matter how brilliant or efficacious, can stand in his way.

They all meet the same end

There is no denying what we read in the book of Ecclesiastes. The "preacher" hits the bull's eye when he calls death the great equalizer. After all, death deals with all human beings in the very same way: they all meet the same end!

And that's why so many react in the same way. They give themselves over to evil and try to live life to the full. In the little time allotted them between the cradle and the grave, they try to get out of life everything they imagine it contains, in the spirit of the old saying "Eat, drink and be merry, for tomorrow we die."

Indeed, for those who do not know better, or do not wish to know better, the cemetery is the place where all men meet the same lot, the place which puts all of them out of action eventually. One person may have been a leading figure during his life while another was a complete unknown, but in the cemetery they are one. Death is death for both of them.

People also tell each other that you have to make your mark during your short stay on earth. Let them know you were here! Enjoy life as long as you can. Be sure to live in the manner that brings you the greatest possible satisfaction.

All human beings — you and I are included — thus live with death before their eyes. Daily we walk in the shadow of death.

No one can escape the moment when he must die. Therefore everything we do, everything we try to accomplish, is fragmentary. Our projects cannot be completed — at least, not by us, for we will not be around forever.

And so, when you think about it carefully you see that what is true of terminal patients is also true for the rest of us. How short life is!

How often it happens that a person leaves his house feeling healthy and glad to be alive — and then never returns alive. Perhaps a traffic accident snuffs out his life. Or a blood vessel bursts in his brain, or he has a massive heart attack.

Terminal? Yes, indeed, everyone's life is coming to an end irrevocably. No one can escape. We all have to reckon with the approach of death.

But do we *really* do so? It is remarkable that so often we play "peek-a-boo" with death. The more that modern man is confronted with death by way of the press and television, the less he wishes to pause and reflect on it. The reality of death is repressed or denied.

When people play this little game there are many who nicely go along with it. Let me give you a small example of what I'm talking about.

He'll get over it, Mother

When I stepped into the spacious hall of the hospital, I saw her sitting there — a simply dressed woman well beyond seventy years of age. She sat in a corner looking lost, tense and nervous.

At first glance she seemed a pathetic figure, and I couldn't help feeling sorry for her. That was also the reason I went up to her and said something. She looked at me sadly and helplessly.

When I asked whether I could sit down by her for a moment, she hesitated in answering. Immediately I sensed that this entire environment was strange to her, and from the conversation that followed, I found that I was right. She came from a small village that was quite some distance from the city. It had taken her more than two hours to get to the hospital, using the bus and the train. It was only the second time she was there: prior to these visits, she had never been inside a hospital.

A week before, her son had been brought to this hospital. The police had come to tell her about it. Her son had had an accident with his motorcycle and had been sent flying. She was told that he had been brought specifically to this hospital, while still unconscious, because it had such fine doctors and medical facilities.

"It's really something strange to me, Sir, this foreign environment," she said. "And then it's so far away from our village. I'm very willing to take the time and spend the money needed for this journey — I do it gladly for my son. He is my only child, and I have been a widow for years already. You can understand how close we are to each other." There were tears in her eyes.

I asked her whether she had already visited her son. Not yet, she told me. The previous time she visited she was told that her son was completely unconscious and was being cared for in a special part of the hospital. It was an area with a special, strange name — where he was watched over separately. "Surely you know what I mean," she said.

I asked her whether she had talked with the doctor. Not yet, she replied. But a nurse had promised to do her best to arrange a visit with the doctor for her the next time she came. "The doctor is so frightfully busy, you know. Now I'm here again, and I'm waiting for the signal."

A nurse summoned her. Somewhat uneasily, she trailed along. She went up one level, to the Intensive Care Unit. I remained seated for a while where I had found her. Perhaps she would return soon.

Some fifteen minutes later she was back. She went right up to me: she was surprised that I was still there. Her attitude was less hesitant, and her eyes did not look as sad anymore. She had perked up somewhat.

"How was it?" I asked gently.

"A gruesome sight," she said. "My son is attached to an apparatus by means of all sorts of tubes — an apparatus that keeps humming and ticking. I hardly got to see anything of him. He is still unconscious. His head is completely wrapped up. Would you believe that the sight of him upset me so much that I couldn't stay there for more than about a minute? . . . But I did get a chance to talk with the doctor!"

"And what did he say?"

"He says it's a very serious case — very complicated, and so forth. But you know what I'm happy about? The doctor *encouraged* me. What he told me made me feel a lot better. He assured me that 'a bear of a fellow' like my son can take a few bumps. And when I took leave of him, he said, 'He'll get over it, Mother.'"

For a moment I stood there perplexed. How did the doctor dare say such a thing to this woman? I said to her, "Let's be thankful that it is God alone who controls life and death. Do you know Him?"

A hard expression came over her face. Suddenly she was in a hurry and said goodbye to me.

That poor woman! What the doctor said seemed to help her more than what I tried to get across.

That same week she was called back suddenly. By the time she arrived at the hospital, her son was dead. He had passed on without ever regaining consciousness. The mother did not get a chance to see him again before he died. She had to rest content with a factual medical explanation: "It was an unexpected complication — the kind of thing that can easily happen. And there was nothing that could be done about it, unfortunately."

Death does not have the last word

We read in Revelation 6:7–8 that the rider on the pale horse is given the power to kill one fourth of the earth. Does this mean that this grim enemy has the last word? Thanks be to God, the answer is No!

If we look carefully at the original text, we see that what is talked about here is not a power that the rider on the pale horse has taken to himself (as a despot or a dictator might do) but an authority that is *conferred* upon him. On his own, then, death is not able to begin anything without getting prior authorization from God.

Now, the authority of the one called death is subordinate to the sovereignty of Christ, who through His death and resurrection overcame the devil, death and hell. By His ascension, Christ received from the Father all power in heaven and on earth. And He uses that power for the good of His Church.

The last word, then, belongs not to death but to the One who has overcome death, who says of Himself: "I am the first and the last and the living One; and I was dead, and behold I am alive forevermore, and I have the keys of death and of Hades" (Rev. 1:17–18).

Enjoying life and work in the shadow of death

From Ecclesiastes 9 we learn that death is the "equalizer." It deals with all human beings in the same way: they all meet the same end.

How does a believer respond to this — someone who, in his heart, confesses that the last word belongs to his Lord and Savior? Does such a believer, through vanity and wantonness, try to repress the thought of death before his eyes?

Never! Just read Ecclesiastes 9:7–9. And bear in mind that what is revealed to us in this passage would never have come from the pen of the "preacher" if he had not known the beautiful promise of the *restoration of life* in the coming Messiah. On the one hand, the "preacher" knew how limited earthly life is, but on the other hand he was aware that through Jesus Christ this (earthly) life will come to its full development in communion with the God of the covenant.

That's why he declares that we may testify of genuine enjoyment in life and an energetic desire to be busy! He mentions some important factors in this connection. Do you know what the LORD demands of you? That in faith you make use of the things He has given you — of eating and drinking, of marriage, and of your daily bread. Just let the sun shine in your life — the joyful light of God's friendly countenance. In Jesus Christ, that light has gone up in your life.

If you do these things, says the "preacher," you are doing what God has long wanted of you. The LORD wants His children to have a *positive* attitude toward life — not a dark pessimism but a joyful optimism.

In verse 10 of chapter 9, the "preacher" says: "Whatever your hand finds to do, verily, do it with all your might; for there is no activity or planning or wisdom in Sheol where you are going."

*   *   *   *   *

Living and working in the shadow of death — with joy and energy. What a wondrous — and at the same time glorious — reality! Now death will no longer strike fear in your heart. Everything that contributes toward your peace has already been done on your behalf by Christ, and this includes everything that gives you and me a measure of security. *We* have also been bought by the LORD. He has paid for us, body and soul — what a comfort!

More Biblical givens

In Chapter 2 I pointed out that the Bible speaks about life and death in three senses. Let's line up these Biblical givens once more.

Natural (biological) life owes its origin, existence and continuation exclusively to God, our Creator. That's why He alone disposes over life and death. Hence we must be very careful with our own life and with the lives of others. If we transgress against life in any sort of self-willed manner, we are violating the seventh commandment ("Thou shalt not kill," Ex. 20:13; Deut. 5:17). In that case we stand condemned before God.

In this connection it is helpful to remember that what we read in Genesis 9:6 is still in effect: "Whoever sheds man's blood, by man shall his blood be shed, for in the image of God He made man." Therefore we read the following statement in Romans 13:4, where the apostle is talking about lawful government: "It does not bear the sword for nothing; for it is a minister of God, an avenger who brings wrath upon the one who practices evil."

Earthly life, then, is not of low value but of very high value. The LORD still watches over it very carefully (Matt. 6:26–30). Life is a gift from Him (Gen. 2:7, 21; Job 10:12). It is very much to be desired (Ps. 34:13) and is intended for the sounding of God's praises (Ps. 8:3; 104:33; 145:2). Earthly life may be enjoyed fully (Eccl. 8:15; 9:7). Our young men and women are even encouraged to enjoy themselves as much as they can in their youth and to gladden their hearts (Eccl. 11:9).

Our natural life is also held in existence by the LORD Himself. Its continuation does not come about automatically. He has bound us to the use of the means which He provides for this purpose. Included among those means are food, clothing and shelter, along with medications and pills. Naturally, when we use these means we must look to God in prayer, in the awareness that His blessing over them is indispensable.

Through our guilt, this earthly life has become what it was not originally — limited, temporary, something to be terminated. Natural death brings an abrupt end to life for many a human being. Death has spread to all men (Rom. 5:12). We can say of death that no mortal will escape its reach. God has decreed that "it is appointed to men to die once, and after this comes judgment" (Heb. 9:27).

For whom is this death terrifying? For those who have lived and died in unbelief. Even though they do not wish to hear anything about death, even though they laugh at the prospect and make a joke of it, *their* death is the irrevocable transition from "spiritual death" to "eternal death."

In John 3:36 we read: "He who believes in the Son has eternal life; but he who does not obey the Son shall not see life, but the wrath of God abides on him." The disobedient person does, of course, share in natural life. He breathes, eats, drinks, and enjoys life among us. But he *remains* what he *is* by nature — dead in trespasses and sins. He will not see life — not now, not ever. A person who does not enjoy communion with God through Christ misses out on real life — eternally, unless he repents. "And if anyone's name was not found written in the book of life, he was thrown into the lake of fire" (Rev. 20:15).

When we bear all of this in mind, we see how privileged believers are. They, too, are by nature dead in trespasses and sins. But they do not remain mired in their sins! Because they are bound to Christ, they share in the righteousness He has achieved through His death. Through His power they are daily awakened to new life. They may continually be assured that His resurrection guarantees *their* resurrection in glory.

It is true — they, too, share in the first, or natural, death. But because they share in Christ's victory, they will "not be hurt by the second death" (Rev. 2:11).

What the Savior says in John 5:24 applies to them: "Truly, truly, I say to you, he who hears My word, and believes Him who sent Me, has eternal life, and does not come into judgment, but has passed out of death into life." We must also take note of what Jesus said to Martha in John 11:25–26. After the death of her brother Lazarus, Martha had indirectly asked him why he did not come earlier, for if He had, her brother would not have died (vs. 21). In His response to her,

Jesus assured her that her brother would arise. Martha assented to this claim, thereby thinking of "the resurrection of the dead" on the last day. But what did the Savior proceed to do? In a striking way He demonstrated that those who believe in Him and thus share in His resurrection when He returns possess eternal life *now*. They will not die. And so he said to Martha: "I am the resurrection and the life; He who believes in Me shall live even if he dies, and everyone who lives and believes in Me shall never die."

Are these mysterious words? Not really, for they confirm what the Bible teaches continually. Thanks to Christ's death and resurrection, the believers already possess the beginning of eternal joy. And a "beginning" is an important part of the whole!

In this context, certain words of Paul are most instructive: "For if we died with Him, we shall also live with Him" (II Tim. 2:11). If we compare this passage with Romans 6:6–11, in which this confession is also found, we see that the words "died with him" refer primarily to "falling asleep in Jesus." In the light of verse 11, we are to think here in terms of dying to our sins in Christ's strength in order to be resurrected to new life. For what we read in this verse is: "Consider yourselves to be dead to sin, but alive to God in Christ Jesus." When you follow the path of genuine conversion, you condemn your sins to death so that you may always continue to live with Christ!

For those who die in faith, death is no longer something to be feared. For them, death represents a radical break with sin, and it forms a transition to eternal life (Heidelberg Catechism, Answer 42).

They are blessed, which is to say that they ought to be heartily congratulated. Through Christ's suffering and death, they have been reconciled with God and have the right to eat of the tree of life and to go through the gates into the city — the eternal Jerusalem (Rev. 22:14).

The unity of life and death

After the preceding Scripture passages, it should no longer seem strange to you that I speak of a *unity* between life and death. I am not taking back anything of what I said earlier. Life and death are not identical and are not to be placed on the same level. They may not simply, or without qualification, be regarded as a unity. But note carefully: "not without qualification." There is more in the picture.

Through His suffering and death, Christ bore the punishment that *we* deserve. Thereby He delivered us from God's curse and from eternal corruption. In Romans 8:1 we read: "There is therefore now no condemnation for those who are in Christ Jesus."

It is important to note that Christ died the "first death" *after* He had already, on Golgotha's cross, died the "second death" (the punishment of hell). Our Mediator had to undergo natural death, as the "wages of sin" (Rom. 6:23), for the justice of God had to be carried out fully in relation to the Son of man.

It is because of this basis that the dying of God's children can take on a totally different character. It is not a repayment for our sins: payment has already been made by Christ. Death no longer includes the sharp sting of God's wrath; because of Christ, it has lost its sting (I Cor. 15:55).

Our dying in Christ is not subject to God's curse, and it enables us to enter eternal joy. Yet for us death does represent a letting go of everything and everyone we love. But the benefit far exceeds the loss. We depart in order to be with Christ always (Phil. 1:23).

We may rest once and for all from our tiring labors in the assurance that our work has not been in vain. Our works follow us (compare Rev. 14:13 with I Cor. 15:58).

At the same time, we are delivered definitively from the consequences of our fall into sin. In the New Jerusalem there will be no inhabitant who says, "I am sick." The people dwelling there have their unrighteousness forgiven (Is. 33:24). God will wipe away all the tears from our eyes, and there will be no more death or mourning or crying or pain, for the first things will have passed away (Rev. 21:4).

We will no longer be hungry or thirsty, nor will the heat of the sun afflict us, for the Lamb in the center of the throne will lead us to pasture and bring us to springs of the water of life, and God will wipe away all our tears (Rev. 7:16–17).

What a glorious reality! For those who, through true faith, have been incorporated into Christ, life and death do not form a sharp *contrast* but a beautiful *harmony*. Now they may already be convinced that nothing — neither life nor death — will be able to separate them from the love of God, which is in our Lord Jesus Christ (Rom. 8:38–39).

It is this conviction of faith, especially, that must activate us when we offer pastoral care to people who are dying. And then it will happen — and not just once — that we, to our joy and encouragement, ascertain that this conviction has become flesh and blood in the seriously ill people we are visiting. Yes, this can happen. Consider the following.

He wanted to remain all by himself

We had known each other for years. It was a spirited, cordial, spontaneous relationship, and we had enjoyed good times together. He loved a joke, and he didn't mind being teased.

Although as a businessman he was always busy, he made time for his wife and children. They were crazy about him. He participated fully in the life of the church. He wanted nothing to do with "black-and-white" thinking, but he wasn't in favor of "evangelical" chatter either. "Just be yourself," he would say, and then you are already crazy enough. In everything he did, he enjoyed himself. He stood in the midst of life — believing, sober, alert, industrious — right up to the time of which I must speak.

On a certain day he telephoned me and said, "Now, don't be frightened, but I have to go to the hospital. According to my doctor, there's nothing to worry about. So don't spread the word around."

The results of the tests in the hospital were disappointing. There was a terminal condition, and it was in an advanced stage. He was allowed to go home to die.

That same week I visited him. It struck me immediately that he and his wife were not depressed. When I expressed my amazement about this, they said, "But aren't we convinced that life with Christ in all of its facets is *eternal*? Well then, the time has come to experience this reality. Surely death will not be an interruption of life with Christ!"

Because I knew them well, I could rest assured that these words were meant in earnest. They were not part of some act being put on by the two of them. Nor were this husband and wife smothering their feelings; on the contrary, they were letting their feelings come out. In a moving manner they said, "Hasn't the LORD said that He will never leave us in the lurch for even a moment? Well then, we shall trust in His power, and hope that we may be able to continue doing so."

In all of this they were not put to shame. The man used the last stage of his life fully. His wife and children cooperated in this effort. I even had to think back to what this friend had once said to me in expressing his own convictions: "The best preparation for death is that you continue serving the LORD — positively, actively, enthusiastically — right up to the time when you draw your last breath." He made this remark years before, when he was healthy. Now it became apparent that it was not cheap talk on his part. As his own death approached, he made it clear that these assurances formed the heart of his own beliefs.

He wanted to experience the *harmony* between life and death. He wanted to show what fruit is borne of reconciliation with God through Jesus Christ.

As much as possible, he wanted to remain himself right up to the last moment — inspired by a living faith. And the LORD granted him his wish. When it came time to take leave of his wife and children, he had a clear mind and was feeling thankful. In these circumstances we see a striking fulfilment of what we read in the Bible: "Blessed is that slave whom his master finds so doing when he comes" (Matt. 24:46; Luke 12:43).

Many people have looked at me with skepticism in their eyes as I told them this story, as if to say, "It's simply too beautiful to be true." My reaction is then: "Let's be thankful that God's *miracles* have not yet disappeared from the world. They are there — if only you have eyes to see them!"

Chapter 4

Death Is Always Lying in Wait

"For soon it is gone, and we fly away . . . So teach us to number our days, that we may present to Thee a heart of wisdom." (Ps. 90:10, 12)

"Man, who is born of woman, is short-lived, and full of turmoil. Like a flower he comes forth and withers. He also flees like a shadow and does not remain." (Job 14:1–2)

"For we know that if the earthly tent which is our house is torn down, we have a building from God, a house not made with hands, eternal in the heavens." (II Cor. 5:1)

Don't forget to live

I remember very clearly walking by a cemetery one day while I was a child. I hardly knew what it was. I looked with respect at the high metal fence with its thick bars. It was too high to climb over, and I couldn't squeeze between the bars either.

I was especially intrigued by the carved letters over the gate, which I was hardly able to make out. They formed words which I didn't understand at all.

At home I was told that the letters above the gate formed the Latin words "Memento mori" (Remember that you must die), which were often used as a sign over the gate to a cemetery. When a person passed such a place, he was supposed to be reminded how short life really is.

And then, suddenly, I understood it all. No more explanation was needed for me to see that I must always avoid such a "place of distress."

Only later did I realize that the sentiment "Remember that you must die" is not Biblical at all. Much better would be the words "Memento vivere" (Remember that you must live). When you look at it from the standpoint of faith, you see that living flows from remembering.

Sometimes adults are just like little children

Recently I met a married couple who had lived opposite a cemetery. My contact with them made me think back to the episode from my youth which I just mentioned.

Being somewhat curious by nature, I wanted to know how these people had liked it there. It turned out to be quite a story: I will keep to the briefer version here. They had only managed to live in their home across from the cemetery for a matter of some months. They couldn't stand it, and no amount of money would induce them to return.

After they had lived there for a month, the trouble began. The children had done some exploring in secret, for they wanted to know what there was to experience in that big, beautiful garden across the street. "Well," said the parents, "we surely did find out.

"When the children returned home, they were bursting with questions. Why were there holes in the ground? Why did people come every now and then and stand around the holes? Why was a box lowered into one of those holes? What was in the box? Why were some of the people crying? And why were others looking so somber?

"Now then, you know how children are. We tried to avoid their questions. Under no condition do you want to talk with your children about dying — it's just not done. You would spoil their lives if you did it!

"Yet our children found out what the place across the street was for. Friends at school told them what was going on. They asked our boys if they didn't find it gruesome to live near a place where so many dead people were lying underground. I'm sure you can understand that when such comments were made, the fat was in the fire. The children came home very upset. They wanted to know whether these things were true.

"The weeks that followed cost us many gray hairs. The children were frightened every time they did as much as look across the street. They wanted to get away — as far as possible from this neighborhood.

"It was very hard on *our* nerves too. We were tense and irritable. It's no fun to see a funeral procession or two pass by your house every day. Such a sight cannot leave you unmoved. Indeed, there were times when we seemed to see *ourselves* riding by on the way to be buried. Now, that's the very last thing you want to think about. Isn't it true? Within half a year we were gone — we had fled!"

It was still for a few moments, as I carefully tried to pick up the threads of what had been said. Naturally, I could understand that these people did not care to live close to a cemetery. On the other hand, a believer need not fear the thought of death.

I did not get any further than that. I was told not to say a word about this matter. They were so happy that they were finally at peace, for now they could enjoy life again. "Therefore, my dear sir, let's remain friends, but please, let's not have any more talk about it."

On the way home I felt somewhat depressed. When you think you have a lot to offer, you are happy to see others benefit from it — all the more so when it is clear just how poor they are.

As I said, I suddenly found myself thinking of my youth. As a mischievous lad I, too, had avoided a cemetery: I took a longer way around. This is the sort of thing a child does naturally.

But God's ordering of our affairs is wise. In later years I extended pastoral care to hundreds of people who were dying. I conducted dozens of funerals in the Netherlands and in other countries as well, where I stood at the open grave and said, "I believe in the resurrection of the body and life everlasting." How could I have foreseen all of this when I was a child?

What struck me about the people I had just met was that on this point they declined to conduct themselves as adults. They still took the long way around to avoid the cemetery — even though they had attained years of discretion long before. How sad!

Sometimes adults are just like little children — children with little wisdom and lots of mischief. Yet they tend to think very highly of themselves.

Death cannot be repressed

There are some things we can learn from this true story. It may be the case that much more has been written and said about death and dying in recent years. Yet the taboo has not been overcome altogether. I know from my own experience that people want to think about death as little as possible. They repress the idea and try to keep it out of their thoughts. Therefore they avoid the places where they would be confronted with this reality. Someone trying to offer pastoral care would do well to acquaint himself with these attitudes. He also needs to know what lies behind them.

In many cases, death is preceded by a period of *suffering* — both spiritual and physical. We should not take this realization lightly. A terminally ill person can be so exhausted and frightened that his feelings can hardly be described. Such exhaustion can have a bad spiritual effect: fear, despair, and even rebellion can take over in the soul of such a person.

Practice shows that what many people dread is not so much the actual *moment* of death as the *process* of death. Because of all that goes with the process of dying, the final phase of life is for many people something frightful. We should not try to belittle people's fears as we talk about death.

Another reality to consider is the feeling of powerlessness in the face of death. As we saw, death is an enemy that cannot be defeated by anything earthly. It defies all medical ingenuity and scientific expertise. This fact strikes fear in the heart of the average man.

Finally, contemporary society is very much geared toward the future. We could speak of it as horizontal in its orientation. On the superficial surface of life, we seem to be concerned with producing and accomplishing more and more. Modern man thinks very highly of development and progress: all forces have to be mobilized to these ends.

In such a society, there is no place for people who are sick, no place for invalids, no place for the dying. Perhaps I should put the point in still stronger terms: in a progressive society in which everything is geared to what we know and are able to do, death is an annoyance, something that does not belong, an undesired intruder. And so, foolish as it may sound, "Death" is declared dead.

Yet death will not allow itself to be repressed. We see death fight back. I think of times when a person is dying but continues to brag and puff himself up. He still yearns for accomplishments and recognition. He still acts as though he is really something. The result is that the process of dying becomes even more difficult for him. If we do not take the time to work through what is happening and learn to accept it calmly, death strikes us like a bomb, causing an enormous explosion and a crater.

Another tragic consequence is that in the face of such an attitude, the family members and others who wish to offer their help are powerless. The person who is dying simply does not allow anyone to help him or even come close to him. Unconsciously, he presents an attitude that keeps people at bay, so that even those who are closest to him find that they do not understand him. They may begin to develop feelings of aversion.

I'm sure you can see that it is refreshing to know that in the church, among believers, death and dying need not be repressed or denied. We can talk about this matter calmly. We do so *because* Christ has shown that the "last enemy" does not have the last word. This joyful message must dominate our interchange with one another and activate our determination to be of help to one another.

The gospel that is proclaimed in church every Sunday fills us all through the week with great joy because it assures us that the oppression of death is taken away for all who believe. Thereby daily life is freed from fear of death and is worth being lived fully.

When we look at things from this point of view, we know that we are obliged to direct our neighbor, who (still) lives in fear, to Christ. In this connection we remember what is written in Hebrews 2:14–15: "He Himself likewise also partook of the same, that through death He might render powerless him who had the power of death, that is, the devil, and might deliver those who through fear of death were subject to slavery all their lives."

Teach us to number our days

These are well-known words. You find them in the prayer of Moses, the man of God (Ps. 90:12). The striking words of this psalm remind us of the frailty of man: he perishes quickly. His life does not last long.

Moses makes this statement in a way that strikes us immediately. Just as a tropical rainstorm in the hilly land of Canaan destroys everything and sweeps it away, so man is carried away by the stream of life. Without even being aware of what is happening, he is carried away in death.

Just as grass on the roof of a house in the Near East may spring up quickly in the early morning but wither in the heat of the afternoon and die, so it is with human life. It does not last long.

What God said directly after the fall into sin applies to every man: "For you are dust, and to dust you shall return" (Gen. 3:19).

It is on man, who is dust, that God's wrath rests. Moses was thinking here of what we read in Numbers 14:26–35. No one can stand before God's holy countenance.

And so life in the wilderness was assigned a set length. At most, people would live to the age of seventy or eighty years. And what did those years deliver? Trouble and disappointment, despite all of man's pushing and slaving and sweating. Often life is more of a burden than a pleasure. Our years fly by, and we fly away with them.

Do these realities lead people to reflect? Do they make them think and turn within? Not at all!

The average man lives as if there is no danger on the horizon. Because he lacks the "fear of God," there is no knowledge of God's strong anger and wrath. People ignore God in the way they live; they act just as if He didn't exist. They do not sense what a terrible thing it is to fall into the hands of the living God (Heb. 10:31).

With these things before his eyes, Moses begged the LORD on behalf of himself and his people for a different posture toward life. He asked for the wisdom that flows from the true fear of the LORD — a wisdom that transcends our understanding. Such wisdom allows us to view the short duration of life in the light of eternity. Thereby it allows us to understand its significance and, in a practical and meaningful way, to live in the light of that understanding.

Teach us to number our days. God must teach us what we, by nature, neither can do nor want to do. This prayer corresponds to what we promise at the baptismal font. In response to this prayer, He fulfils His promise through His Word and Spirit.

*   *   *   *   *

The result is far-reaching. With Moses we affirm that the LORD has been our refuge from generation to generation. Thanks to the favor He has shown us, we have not perished. There is no end to His mercies: every morning they are new. Great is God's faithfulness (Lam. 3:22–23).

Indeed, through living covenantal fellowship, the work of our hands is established by the LORD, our God. The manifestations of His love are like sunshine in our lives. What a blessing! As we count our days, we learn to count God's blessings — one by one.

A building made by God, an eternal house

We live out our life on earth between the delivery room and the deathbed. It is only a short period. For many it is filled with anguish.

Job could tell you all about it. During the period in which he was being tempted by the devil and tested by God, there were some moments when it was simply too much for him. He saw no light at the end of the tunnel. In Job 14:1–2, we find certain words in which Job characterized the situation of man as he had come to regard it. His days are few, and he is full of turmoil. Like a flower, he blossoms, but soon he withers. He does not remain on the scene for long.

If you live day by day in the small circle of a family with a terminally ill patient, you will be able to understand Job's reaction very well. And the experiences of doctors, nurses and aides in hospitals and nursing care facilities also underscore what we read in the book of Job. They see so much sorrow and suffering — and God's children are not exempted.

We must not forget that believers often receive a *double* portion of such troubles while they are in this "vale of tears." As they struggle to come to terms with their physical — and sometimes also mental — degeneration, they may well run into serious difficulties with their "experience" of faith. It has often struck me that when you get older, the doubts begin to creep into your mind, even for those who used to have both feet right on the ground, spiritually speaking.

The real doubt often does not concern the faithfulness of God but the extent to which the doubting person has been faithful in return. And the earnestness of such painful doubts cannot easily be overestimated. If the doubts are not quickly recognized for what they are and dealt with in an appropriate manner, the patient can unwittingly fall into an ever deeper spiritual morass. Be very careful on this score. There are so many misunderstandings that can lead to a "breakdown."

Now, in a certain sense we may be pleased that people doubt their own faithfulness. Nowadays you don't run into such feelings all that often — the opposite is more likely to prove a problem.

Such doubts can be grounded in a genuine sense of one's own unworthiness. If so, they testify to a self-knowledge which is indispensable for those who take refuge in Christ and make an appeal to God's faithfulness.

This is a familiar matter: it is when we possess true knowledge of our misery that we seek and find our security and joy outside of ourselves in Jesus Christ. If you point this out to the one who is doubting, you are not leaving him in darkness; rather, you are offering him your hand in support and helping him get secure on the only foundation for our salvation.

In this context I would point to what we read in II Corinthians 5:1, where the apostle Paul compares our short-lived existence to a tent.

Now, a tent represents *temporary* shelter: it is light in weight and easy to use. It is ideal for those who are traveling by bicycle on their vacation. In a minimum of time you can set up your shelter for the night, and in the morning the tent is quickly packed up, leaving you ready to move on. No great effort on your part is required.

The earthly tent in which we live is continually subject to "breakdown." The process begins at the time of conception, and it advances every day of our life. But it does not go ahead at the very same speed in every person, nor is everyone equally hard hit by the process of decay. But for everyone the process eventuates in death. And then what?

In this context I must speak from the heart and say that I believe we can never thank the LORD enough for His liberating gospel. It is because of the gospel that we who are of the church know that the taboo regarding death and dying has been broken through — all because of Easter, the resurrection of our Lord Jesus Christ.

The basic break between life and death has been healed for those who believe. This means that the answer to the question "And then what?" was already given many centuries ago — by the One who overcame death and enabled true life to triumph.

On this basis we see that we need *not* doubt what awaits us when our earthly tent is rolled up. We do not cease to exist. We live further, even though our body is buried and returns to dust. For we have a building from God, in the heavens, one that is not made with hands — an eternal house.

Our new life began with the resurrection of our Lord. It was His death that prepared such life for us, a life that will endure into eternity.

A rich life gave her a calm deathbed

The sorrows and difficulties of life had not been spared her. If we measure by the yardstick of this world, she was indeed a woman to be pitied. She never married, and she had almost no family. All her life long she had to work hard just to keep her head above water. This cost her great disappointment. And she was not strong: ever since childhood, her constitution had been weak.

When I met her for the first time, she was already elderly. She lived in a rather poor neighborhood. Her house was small, and its furnishings modest. But she kept it very clean. From everything, one could see that she had not had an easy life. The people in the neighborhood admitted that she was hard up.

When I visited her, I was struck by the fact that she was not only friendly but content. She had the coffee ready, and she assured me repeatedly that she was glad I had come. And I could declare in return that it gave me pleasure to meet her.

We had a good conversation. It appeared that she came from a family of socialists. Neither at school nor at home did she have any Christian background. While she was quite young, she served as a maid in the home of a Reformed family, and there she came into contact with the gospel. She made confession of her faith and was baptized in the congregation to which she still belonged.

She was happy that she had become a Christian. She couldn't get over the happiness her faith had brought her. From our conversation it was evident that she followed church events carefully and was well informed. She enjoyed the preaching every Sunday. She regarded it as a fine thing to be completely accepted among the brothers and sisters of the church. In the church she was not looked down on. Even though she was poor in material and financial respects, spiritually she felt richer than a king. And that remained her attitude — even when her earthly tent was slowly but surely being rolled up.

The last months she was not able to rise from her bed. I could see her bodily strength diminishing. She got thinner and thinner; she was like a candle burning down to the wick. Every day, members of the congregation came to help her. She was very thankful for their assistance. I'm pleased to say that she kept a clear mind to the end. My pastoral visits were a pleasure for us both.

Repeatedly I joined her in thanking the LORD for the riches she received from His hand. She yearned for the moment when she would be set free in order to be with Christ. Even when she could hardly speak any more, her eyes shone with her joy in the Lord. It was a pleasure for me to behold her happiness.

On the very last day, when she felt she was about to die, she asked me to read II Corinthians 4:16 through 5:10. She lay there relaxed and calm while I read, murmuring her assent. Gladly she added her amen: from God she would receive an eternal house — with Him!

The *riches* of her life gave her a *calm* deathbed. I saw many members of the congregation at her funeral. Around the open grave we could sing gratefully: "Thy mercies rise up and form an arch — an ever secure house, firm as heaven itself" (Psalm 89).

Chapter 5

Openness Needed

"And this I pray, that your love may abound still more and more in real knowledge and all discernment."

(Phil. 1:9)

"Pray for us, for we are sure that we have a good conscience, desiring to conduct ourselves honorably in all things." (Heb. 13:18).

"Now may the God of peace Himself sanctify you entirely; and may your spirit and soul and body be preserved complete, without blame at the coming of our Lord Jesus Christ" (I Thess. 5:23)

Keep differences in mind

People differ a great deal from one another. They differ in many respects — in their basic natures, in what they can comprehend, in their disposition, and in their feelings.

That's why two people in virtually the same situation may react in strikingly different ways. Those differences become even more manifest when the power of resistance is weak, as is the case among people who are seriously ill or are dying. But this phenomenon is not limited to such people; it also manifests itself among those who spend much of their time offering assistance to such needy people and who thereby come under a great deal of tension themselves.

From both sides this must be taken into account if the help we offer is to be effective. If we do not have a good sense of one another's situation, we can easily get bogged down in misunderstandings. There can be conflicts that stand in the way of a relationship

53

in which we open our hearts to one another. When this happens, much is spoiled. Let me explain a little further.

The healthy and the sick cannot get along without each other

In the church, the sick and the dying do not form a separate category that can more or less be written off. They are not to be regarded as people on the sidelines.

They are the ones most in need of our special care and continuing help. Think of what is revealed in I Corinthians 12:24–27.

In order that we may practice the communion of saints effectively, we must pay attention to how God has structured the body that is the Church. He gives more honor to those who are destitute. Why? So that there will be no division within the body: instead, the members will care and provide for one another on an equal basis.

The result is nothing short of amazing. It becomes apparent within the communion of believers that if one person is suffering, all are suffering along with him, and if one person is honored, all share the joy with him.

That's the way it ought to be in the church when it comes to those who are sick and those who are well. After all, are we not the body of Christ and thus members of one another?

Those who are suffering in physical and/or mental respects thus have a right to our compassion — for the sake of Christ. They are our travel companions on the pathway to salvation. This applies in special measure to God's children who almost have the last part of the journey behind them, the ones who, in the foreseeable future, may be expected to depart for their Father's House. When we consider the tensions they have to live with, we realize that they must have a special need of our heartfelt concern.

We should not simply take their complaints about feeling lonely and isolated as information. Such complaints have to be looked at seriously. When these people appeal to our pastoral mercy, it must not be in vain.

But there is another side to this matter. It is difficult to be responsible in our dealings with people who are terminally ill. An appropriate training for such work is needed, along with an attitude that is attuned to the purpose. To be knowledgeable in this area means to understand more deeply and to help more effectively. It is very important to study the better literature in this field.

Every human being has his own character and personality. But in the face of death, one's personality can be so completely changed or deformed that the person becomes unrecognizable even to the family members who are closest to him or her. The field of tensions to which he is exposed can have a negative influence in this respect.

One must know how to react to such changes. If we are to be sympathetic and genuinely helpful in such circumstances, we must have some knowledge of the physical and psychological changes which the illness causing death brings about.

The reactions and conduct of cancer patients differ somewhat from those of patients suffering from heart ailments, lung diseases or nervous afflictions. It is clear that there is some sort of psychosomatic interaction between a person's emotional make-up and the nature of his disease or affliction.

A person who wishes to offer pastoral help must not become irritated or disappointed when a more pleasant and meaningful contact with a patient is possible on one day in contrast with another. If we are careful and follow sensible policies, we will still be able to help our fellow human being who is suffering. We can help him maintain the right relationship to God, to himself and to his surroundings. After all, we are personally drawn into his situation because our fall into sin makes us jointly responsible for the consequences of that fall.

Healthy people and sick people cannot get along without each other. They are travel companions on the one path that is being followed by the Church of Christ. Thus they must help and support one another, secure in the knowledge that He who, for the sake of Christ, is our God and Father continues to hold our right hand. He leads us in accordance with His counsel in order, one day, to take us up into glory!

Abounding in real knowledge and all discernment

This is what the apostle Paul wishes for his readers in Philippians 1:9–10. It is a joy for him to see how tight the bond is between them and him. Therefore he expresses the wish that the reciprocal love may abound ever more. Such a warm attitude toward one another is indispensable if we, in all sorts of areas and in the face of all circumstances, are to show ourselves to possess the clear insight that Paul calls real knowledge, along with what he calls discernment. Both of these are necessary if we are to be practical and responsible in the way we act. True love enhances our vision, clarifies our thinking, strengthens our capacities, and refines our powers of observation.

What is described here is precisely what we need if we are to be truly helpful to people who are dying of terminal illnesses. It is clear that our pastoral concern for them can get us into situations in which much wisdom, empathy and patience are demanded. We can only manage all of this if we are willing to give of ourselves without holding anything back, that is, if we really show the dying person that we are *with* him or her, so that we do not seem at the same moment — if only in part — to be concerned with matters of our own. When we lose ourselves in our own thoughts, we may well sit by the bed of a dying person for a whole hour without really giving the sick person a few minutes of our attention.

If we are to make time free for the people who need our help, we must make ourselves available fully and honestly. When people do this, they encounter one another as sinners who are together placed before the reality of death and dying. To be truly sympathetic means to feel the suffering of the other person along with him.

This kind of sympathy is something different than the attitude which a healthy person sometimes takes, that is, when he or she looks at the suffering person from a standpoint of supposed safety. It is different from looking at a dying person as a poor "sucker" who has to be treated with pity.

Such a condescending attitude represents a denigration of the person in question. If, in such a manner, the patient becomes a victim of our supposed charity, we are offending him. He then has to be satisfied with a handout from us, which is offered to him as though it were a tip. If this is our approach to the sick and dying, we should be ashamed of ourselves!

A truly Scriptural concern that guides your approach to the other person in his need for help will lead you to make an effort to allow him to share in *God's* mercy. Thus our help represents a positive deed of faith! Through such a deed, we show how much we desire to "abound in real knowledge and all discernment." When we take such an approach, we see clearly what it is all about and act in a way that is truly helpful to those who are entrusted to our care.

Wanting to follow the right path in all respects

This emphasis flows naturally from the preceding one. Giving pastoral help to people who are dying of terminal illnesses is difficult and responsible work. Therefore we should remember the pastoral workers in our prayers. The issue is that they must be able to do their work in a careful manner. And they need to have a clear conscience in relation to God and their neighbor. Their conscience will be clear if in all respects (thus also in the way they offer their assistance) they walk the path that is responsible and right before God. You can read about this in Hebrews 13:18.

In this context I should yet say the following. In order to understand your neighbor, you must try to feel what he is feeling as much as you can. This does not mean that his feelings literally become yours: such a thing is not possible. And we must be careful not to identify ourselves with people who are dying; we have to remain who we are. Thus we have to stand above our work, but without coming across to people as distant.

Since we can never take over the suffering of others, the proper attitude is to remain *faithful* to our calling. If we do this, we are being reliable, and the person we are helping has someone to hold on to, someone he can talk with confidentially, someone who lends him support. If the dying cannot rely fully on the faithfulness of those who come to help them, their sense of being alone becomes even more acute.

Naturally, our faithfulness is sometimes put to the test — perhaps it is severely tested. After all, we are dealing with sinful people, and we are sinners ourselves. And it is important to ask ourselves continually how *we* would conduct ourselves in similar circumstances.

The ideal, then, is to follow the right path, to be faithful, and to have a clear conscience. We must be deeply aware of the necessity of all of this when we answer the question whether people who are suffering from terminal illnesses need to be told exactly how serious their situation is in medical respects.

People do not all think alike on this question. Some decades ago it was regarded as wrong to tell a patient that his illness was terminal. During the early years of my pastoral work I have more than once experienced that doctors were strongly opposed to open communication on this score.

The following practical cases will speak for themselves.

He could no longer restrain himself

She was only thirty-eight years old when she fell ill. She had four children and had always been a capable woman who enjoyed life. But now she was always tired. Her family doctor took up contact with a specialist. He examined her and had her admitted to the hospital. After the necessary tests, it was decided to operate on her stomach.

She was tense as she looked ahead to the operation, which was to be performed on a Thursday. Her husband was at her bedside in good time that day. He wanted to encourage her before the operation. I had visited her the day before and had discussed my visit with her husband. They were a brave couple, depending fully on the LORD

When the operation was over, the husband was called in by the specialist, from whom he then heard the distressing news that his wife had only a few more months to live. A malignant swelling in her stomach had resulted in the spread of the cancer all over her body. There was not much more that could be done about it. But it was emphasized to this man that he was to say nothing to his wife about it. To tell her the news would be irresponsible!

That same day he was given an opportunity to visit his wife. When he entered her room, she was already conscious and lay there waiting for him. Happily and thankfully she said, "Isn't it wonderful that it's all behind us, and that with God's help I can now get better quickly?"

At that moment the man could no longer restrain himself. While he turned around and reached for his handkerchief, he sobbed out the truth. His wife understood at once. "Then it's incurable?" she asked gently. He nodded. But when the specialist found out, he was furious.

Under no circumstances are you to tell her

In such a case, a pastor can get caught in the crossfire. He will have to act wisely and make a decision, as I have found out from experience. Consider the following.

An elderly sister of the congregation had been taken into the hospital for an operation. When it was over, her husband came to inform me of the outcome. As soon as he walked in, I knew what he had come to say.

The doctors had given up on his wife. Her condition was very critical, her cancer was in an advanced stage. This sad news was followed by an urgent appeal to me as the minister to pass on the news to the man's wife. He regarded it as necessary for her to know the truth if their remaining time together was to be meaningful. He was sure she would receive the news calmly.

I said yes to this request. I decided that before I called on the woman, I should contact the doctor handling the case. He had to be informed of my intention.

I went to the hospital and asked a porter if I could get in touch with Dr. X to talk with him for a moment. It turned out that he was not at the hospital, but he could be reached by telephone. The well-meaning porter dialed the number for me himself.

I informed the doctor briefly what I was planning to do, and why I regarded this as the best course to follow. His answer was: "Under no circumstances are you to tell her. I will take the ultimate responsibility for this decision."

We could not come to agreement. Even so, I honored the brother's request. And I was all the more determined to go ahead when I noted in the course of my conversation with the sister that she wanted to be informed honestly. To this day I am thankful that I went ahead.

Yet I brought down the displeasure of the specialist on my head. In part because I was open with the sister, this married couple was able to enjoy a short but meaningful time of preparation for the departure that lay ahead — under the blessing of the LORD.

The doctor in this case simply did not want to understand it. To each his own responsibility — this is what I would say in response to him.

He simply did not wish to know

He was a rather unusual man — somewhat closed and preoccupied with himself. He worked hard and provided well for his wife and children. But beyond this I could find out little about him. He did not express himself to anyone about his spiritual life. Not even his wife knew "how it stood with him."

Suddenly he had to be brought to the hospital. The tests indicated that a rather serious operation was needed. You could not easily tell what was going through this brother's mind. He was even more closed than otherwise.

Before the operation took place, he instructed the specialists and the other medical personnel dealing with his case not to tell him about his illness. He simply did not wish to know!

His request was honored by all concerned. Ultimately the wishes of a patient need to be respected, even by people who shake their heads over the situation.

What a strange man: one does not often run into such a case. The way matters unfolded is well worth our attention.

For a number of weeks, there was not a word about the "hot potato" during my pastoral visits with him. I was wondering how long we should and could stay away from the subject. Finally, he himself broke the taboo.

One day he began to talk. He said that he found it remarkable that everyone was silent about the nature of his illness. This he regarded as a bad sign.

I pointed out to him that this silence was his own doing. He was still for a moment, apparently trying to get control of himself. And then it happened. He began to talk freely with me, opening his heart. The ice had been broken. He admitted that he had been playing a game of cat and mouse because he suspected he would not live long anymore. He had chosen to repress the reality of the situation. He admitted that he was guilty on this score, also in his relationship to his wife and children.

From the one day to the other he had changed. And the LORD even gave him some good times with his loved ones before he died. They made good use of their time together. Did the change come about at the eleventh hour? Yes, but that was still in time, thanks to God's great mercy. To Him alone be the glory!

Don't establish universal rules

In recent years, people have become somewhat more flexible with regard to these things — to the point that there is some danger of going too far in the opposite direction. There are medical people now who believe that a terminal patient has to be told flatly that he will die before long.

It is my conviction that we must not lay down *universal* rules when it comes to this matter. As long as the patient does not know how serious his situation is, one must be very careful, especially if the patient seems to sense something of the truth but does not express it.

But such uncertainty should not be allowed to last for long. Continuing doubt can have a bad effect; it can consume the patient.

More than once I have heard people I visited in the hospital say that there is nothing worse than uncertainty. They would rather be told exactly what their situation is, medically speaking.

But in such a case, too, one would have to be careful. Someone who is very seriously ill can look brave and say that he wants to hear the truth, whereas the result of telling him is that he takes a turn for the worse and demonstrates that he was not ready for the truth after all. Someone offering pastoral assistance must therefore be very sensitive when making decisions about this matter. He must be able to sense whether the person to whom he is ministering is staying away from the difficult questions, as opposed to having them answered in order to attain peace. If concern or anxiety is left unexpressed, the tension in a person's situation can increase until it becomes unbearable.

But does a sick person always have the right to know just what the medical situation is? Some would answer this question with an unqualified yes, but I would offer a somewhat more nuanced answer. We must consider carefully with whom we are dealing. What is the patient's condition? Is he able to handle a shocking communication?

Therefore to me it seems necessary to take some responsibility when it comes to this matter. Naturally, this must be done in consultation with the family and the attending physician. A cooperative relationship between a family, a pastor, and a doctor who all share the same faith convictions is the ideal and is very good for the patient. To this I can testify from my own experience.

Preserved complete, without blame

This is what must touch the hearts of God's children! What a privilege to have this perspective before you constantly in this busy, hurried life! What a blessing to possess such an assurance as you lie on your deathbed!

Who is it, then, that preserves us unto eternal life? Who is it that sees to it that on the day of Christ's appearing we will be "preserved complete, without blame?" In I Thessalonians 5:23 we get the answer to this question. Your preserver is the God of peace, the source and finisher of your reconciliation with Him.

We beg Him to protect and watch over His children, and then in such a way that we are not subjected to decay so that we will reach our glorious final destiny. We are sanctified by God — which is to say that we are set apart as the people of His choosing. We are preserved whole and complete.

To ask these things in prayer makes good sense and is by no means a waste of time. We may plead on the basis of the oath which the LORD swore to us at the time of our baptism. Drawing on the familiar form for baptism, we could say that the Holy Spirit "imparts to us what we have in Christ, namely, the cleansing from our sins and the daily renewal of our lives." In this way we will ultimately enter eternal life completely clean and receive a place in the midst of the congregation of those whom God has chosen.

It seems clear to me that this hope — expressed in all simplicity and openness — is what we must hold before God's children when they are preparing to die. When we do so, we are offering Biblical, pastorally responsible care!

The fruit of such help to the dying will surely be something outstanding. I have experienced this truth many times myself. A salutary rest came over the dying person. Just as he had drawn strength and courage from God's promises throughout his life, so he continued to do in the face of death.

Here we see confirmed what is expressed so clearly in Psalm 23: "Even though I walk through the valley of the shadow of death, I fear no evil; for Thou art with me; Thy rod and Thy staff, they comfort me."

The LORD our God watches over His own who seek Him in prayer. As His mercy covers us, we may build on the firm foundation of His promises and His covenant.

Chapter 6

A Crisis Situation

"I would have despaired unless I had believed that I would see the goodness of the LORD in the land of the living. Wait for the LORD; be strong, and let your heart take courage; yes, wait for the LORD."

(Ps. 27:13–14)

"I have fought the good fight, I have finished the course, I have kept the faith; in the future there is laid up for me the crown of righteousness, which the Lord, the righteous Judge, will award to me on that day; and not only to me, but also to all who have loved His appearing." (II Tim. 4:7–8)

"Be faithful until death, and I will give you the crown of life." (Rev. 2:10)

Phases in the process of dying

There are a number of things to bear in mind when we look after the dying. Not only do they, as people, differ from one another in general, but the course run by their respective illnesses may differ considerably day by day and from case to case. Therefore it is not enough for us to equip ourselves with knowledge and expertise: our knowledge must be paired with sensitivity and practical wisdom. We must, as it were, know *how* to act or intervene at a certain, often critical, moment — and then in such a way that the effect is salutary.

This comment applies especially to those who offer *pastoral* help. In changing situations, a great deal is asked of such people. And I believe that these high expectations are justified when we bear in mind what they, on Christ's behalf, may pass on to the people they serve.

It goes without saying that I had a great deal to learn when it comes to offering pastoral care to people who are seriously ill. I am happy to pass on something of what I have learned, supplemented with examples where necessary.

People suffering from terminal illnesses find themselves in a situation of crisis. Their illness has taken a decisive turn. Because of this turn and some other factors as well, there is a major change in their lives.

There are a number of phases in the process of dying. It is good to be aware of these phases, provided that such knowledge is not used in a purely theoretical or distantiated way.

From experience we learn that our emotional response to the process of dying is not to be understood as a level, uniform schema. There is no general rule that is applicable to every situation or every dying person. The moods which manifest themselves — sometimes even in the life of one and the same person — are too various for such a general pattern to be accepted as universal.

Moreover, those emotions and feelings are experienced within a field of tension which, in its temporal duration and intensity, corresponds to the unfolding of a process. Indeed, it is even somewhat dependent on that process.

A tense uncertainty

The *first* phase is characterized by the moment when the patient becomes aware of just how serious his ailment is. It is not easy to discern exactly when this takes place: in many cases the moment escapes our observation. A person who is ill may harbor dark suspicions for a long time without ever discussing them with anyone. The reality of the situation does not penetrate immediately. The eventual realization may begin with a vague preliminary feeling that something is seriously wrong.

Some people, depending on how much they are able to comprehend, may concentrate their observation very strongly on themselves.

They pay careful attention to what they think they are hearing from the specialist and the nurses dealing with them. It is especially in this initial period that we see a tense uncertainty.

This uncertainty must not be allowed to continue for very long. I believe it is the specialist who is primarily all responsible for bringing it to an end. He has many diagnostic tools at his disposal, and he knows what the course of the disease in question usually is. He is also in a good position to judge to what extent he should let the patient know the facts of the matter.

It does not seem right to me that in many cases the close family members or the pastor are informed *before* the patient himself. When this is done, the result can all too easily be that improper relationships come to stand in the way of optimal pastoral care. If possible, *the doctor* should inform the sick person, perhaps drawing in the pastor at this point, so that the latter can offer direct support. I know from my own experience that such teamwork can be very effective.

Once the reality of the situation is brought home to someone who is seriously ill, there are various phenomena that may present themselves by way of reaction. They range from denial to a refusal to pay attention to the matter. The initial shock may be so powerful that the patient is completely floored by it. But soon he tries to recover: he pulls himself together and shows himself to be somewhat active.

In any case he tries to deny the basic fact. He talks about something else, or perhaps he trivializes his illness. He says he'll be over it before long. But as soon as he is alone, he has to look the realities in the face: there is no longer any reason to hide the facts.

It is clear that the terminal patient in this stage must grow in the direction of coming to terms with the reality of his situation. We have to make sure we give him the time to do so; we have to be willing to talk with him in an understanding way. Every signal to which we respond can be of interest and can help us come to a proper conclusion, so that we can be effective in the help we offer the patient. One must indeed be diligent!

Powerlessness seeks a way out

In the *second* phase the terminal patient tries to recover his balance. Often this phase is paired with still greater tensions. The feeling of powerlessness often leads to resistance. More than once we may find the patient becoming apathetic or even rebellious. There may be a number of emotional storms or outbursts of wrath. The patient may strike out at close family members or even at his or her spouse. In many cases he takes it out on the doctor or the pastor.

In the most favorable cases, the anger, passion or irritation may give way to a crying fit. Usually the patient will feel somewhat better afterward.

It is important for us to know what to do in such a situation. One must remain calm and not strike back at the patient emotionally. Such a reaction would do no good, and it is unfair.

Powerlessness is looking for an outlet. If you are the one at whom the patient blows off steam, you should not feel offended or picked on. The patient is not attacking you personally; rather, he is seeking a release for the emotions raging within him.

It is a wise policy to approach such a person in need with tact and understanding. Just let him feel that you, too, are powerless in the situation. In many cases this will help. Wait for an opportunity to talk about certain difficulties. And when you bring in the Scriptures, you can be assured in advance that you are not wasting your breath. It has been my own repeated experience that both the dying person and his family need to be approached in a pastoral way. Use the same manner that you would use in dealing with someone who is ill.

What you should bear in mind especially is that no one is helped by empty generalities. But Scriptural encouragement and comfort never stop having an effect — even if the words of encouragement need to be repeated a number of times.

Let me give you a practical example to clarify this second phase. The wife of a terminal patient to whom I was ministering came to my study to unburden herself. She was feeling downcast, and she understood nothing of what she was suffering. Throughout the years, her marriage had been a very happy one. She and her husband had always understood one another very well, and when troubles had come along, they knew how to deal with them. Truly, their relationship was ideal!

But she could not deal with what had happened recently. Not long before, her husband had been informed that he was suffering from an incurable disease and that he would be dead before long. He had demanded to know the truth, and the doctor told him.

At first he accepted it in a more or less passive manner. The two of them were able to talk about it calmly during the hour I spent visiting them. Each could sense how difficult it was for the other. They had promised each other that they would help one another in God's strength. He had even said, "It's a fine thing that we can prepare *together* for our coming separation. After all, we know to whom we are to look to for comfort." Our conversation had done them both some good.

Because of this beginning, the situation she walked into a week later was all the more painful. She did not recognize her husband: hardly had she sat down next to his bed when he attacked her in a manner that was anything but pleasant. All kinds of accusations were thrown at her. She did not know how to respond. Deeply disappointed and somewhat irritated, she went back home.

An hour later she came to see me. She was disappointed, upset, and rather angry. Why was such treatment being meted out to her? Did she deserve it? Naturally, I let her talk at first. I listened carefully, paying special attention to her posture.

When she was finished, I said, "Madame, at that moment you were given distinct proof of how very *deeply* your husband loves you."

She looked at me in amazement. By way of explanation, I then went on to tell her that it happens more often that terminal patients, in the effort to deal with the situation in which they find themselves, react aggressively toward the person they love most. It's not that they want to quarrel or be unfair, but they have to blow off steam because of the enormous tension under which they live. And who better to blow up at than the person they trust more than any other?

This short explanation seemed to clarify things for the woman. Through God's grace it proved possible to work things out in such a way that this married couple, despite this stormy episode, managed to get to the final stage of the man's illness in full dependence on the

LORD. It turned out that they were able to be of tremendous comfort and support to one another during the most difficult time of their life. And they received pastoral support in the name of Christ.

Making a deal

During the *third* stage it can happen that the dying person takes on an attitude that amazes us. At times when he is feeling a little better, hope revives in him. He tries to be brave and even makes plans for the future. He tries to make a deal with himself. He thinks to himself, "Doctors can make mistakes, and so it wouldn't be the first time that someone who was given up for dead went on to live for many years."

Usually such a "revival" does not last long. And when it takes place, we must be ready at every moment for what is likely to follow, namely, a sinking back. Inevitably there comes a turn, and then our help is needed. If God does not prevent it, the patient may be even worse off than before; indeed, things may go so far that he feels he has been forsaken by both God and man.

His silence and his desire to be alone may go so far that he no longer values visits. And it should not surprise a pastor that talking about the LORD, reading the Bible and praying will irritate the patient at that point. If this happens, you should not make an issue of it. The *personal* prayers you continue to raise on behalf of such patients are never in vain. And there will come moments when they are thankful for your continuing personal interest in them. After all, our God does not let go of the works of His hands. *He* holds on to His children with His right hand.

Giving up hope

For family members and for those who offer assistance to the dying, it can be painful to watch a dying person fall silent and seem to lose hope. Even more difficult to deal with is the hopelessness that is associated with the *fourth* phase. When such hopelessness manifests itself, there is virtually nothing that can be done for the patient. Of course this does not mean that the pastor ceases to visit him. But he needs to understand that there is not much he can do about the depression he now encounters. We can be thankful that this situation usually does not last long.

All of a sudden there can be a moment when the silent patient feels the need to talk again. When such a moment comes in my ministry, I am deeply grateful that I may be an instrument in God's hand to be of help.

What may also happen is that the sadness is lessened and the fear of death vanishes. Of course the patient looks back over episodes in his life with some degree of wistfulness, knowing that his life must now come to an end. We should not try to suppress such feelings. On the contrary, we must show ourselves willing to talk about the old days and thereby help the dying person toward acceptance. When you do this, your loving care for the terminal patient makes his burden lighter.

At such moments there can also come an opportunity to confront a dying person who is not a believer with the gospel. In my own experience I have sometimes found a willing ear at this point. Most of the time, however, the patient will not want to listen. Of course this does not mean that you should then "remain neutral."

Acceptance

The *fifth* stage (usually the last one) is characterized by a definitive acceptance of impending death. For believers this can be a beautiful time. We can say that life on earth is being rounded off. It is then possible to talk peacefully with family and friends about one's life. In many cases the faith of the family members and close friends and associates of the dying person is strengthened because of what happens during this stage. We see an openness that was not present before.

We find that children who are still in the process of growing up when this happens can recall such moments clearly many years later. What a blessing for their lives such preparation can be! It is striking that this stage does not appear to be an ordeal for the family. The children can even laugh along with the father or mother who is dying, although this does not mean that the gravity of the situation is then forgotten.

When this stage comes, the visits of the pastor are eagerly welcomed. They also turn out to be stimulating and refreshing for the pastor himself.

In this last stage, the gospel has a great deal to offer the dying person, provided he still has a clear mind. I have often been struck by how a sentence from Scripture or a well-known psalm can bring light to the face of a terminally ill patient. I find that in such cases all sorts of feelings run through me. You feel like crying out to everyone you meet: "I would have despaired unless I had believed that I would see the goodness of the LORD in the land of the living." Therefore we have all the more reason to say: "Wait for the LORD; be strong, and let your heart take courage; yes, wait for the LORD" (Ps. 27:13–14).

Fight the good fight and keep the faith

These words from II Timothy 4:7–8 meant a great deal to a brother whom I visited for a while when he was dying. We had known each other for years and had become very good friends. We had stood shoulder to shoulder during a time in the Netherlands when Reformed church life had come under attack in a contemptible way. During that period he had shown that he was an elder you could depend on. He had steered the right course, remaining calm and resolute, not forgetting his compass, not allowing anyone or anything to lead him astray.

The deathbed of this brother was something remarkable and worth discussing. After he was told that his illness was fatal, he still tried to do as much as he could for his family and congregation. The doctor urged him strongly to cease his daily work and to live very calmly. He followed this advice. Yet he was able to persuade the doctor that he was simply not the kind of man who can be rendered altogether inactive. As long as it was not necessary, he wanted to stay away from the sidelines. And so he secured the doctor's permission to be active — in a measured way — for his family and the congregation.

This period lasted for about a year. One cannot help but respect what our brother meant to those around him during this period. People still talk about it with appreciation, for it was indeed remarkable.

Although he became steadily weaker and one could see that he was in pain, he kept going. He kept a close eye on all the developments in his own family, his circle of friends, and his congregation. He kept himself informed, and his heart went out to others. He wanted to die "in harness."

The LORD granted this wish. Right to the very end, he remained in active service, even when he could no longer rise from his bed.

I visited him every week. His mind remained clear, even though long conversations tired him out. During the final weeks he pointed especially to the apostle Paul. He had been struck by the rich grace extended to this brother. "If you read in II Corinthians 11:23 what this brother endured," he said, "you are amazed at all the things he had to suffer, and you wonder how he escaped with his life."

All of this was a clear indication of God's grace, which had been sufficient for Paul and would also be enough for our brother. He expressed it openly: thanks to this gift of God, he could remain active those last months, despite all his pain and weariness. For him there was reason to be thankful that he was able to fight the good fight and keep the faith. Great was the LORD's mercy toward him.

On the day of his death, his wife and children were seated near his bed. I was present as well. The last moments were impressive. He could still make himself clearly heard as he assured the members of his family that the crown of righteousness lay ready for him too. "And also for you who love Christ's appearing," he added immediately. "Hold on to that assurance throughout your life." He gestured once more with his hand, saying goodbye to all of us.

Was this an exceptional death? In a certain sense it was. In any event, it is not to be denied that it is a token of God's unending mercy toward those who know they are lost sinners. You and I must now rely on that mercy — every day. But you understand, of course, that things do not always go in just the way described in this case. Consider the next one.

She wanted so much to go on living

She was admitted to the hospital because of a nasty tumor. At the time I did not know whether she realized how serious her condition was. As I became acquainted with her, I got the impression that she was convinced that her stay in the hospital would be a short one. Expert medical attention would soon have her on her feet again.

She clung stubbornly to this conviction during the two months that were left to her. All who took care of her and ministered to her found it a painful situation. The doctor had given her the facts, but she did not react to them. As pastor I tried to use every visit to prepare her for the end that was coming. She listened carefully and nodded when I read aloud from the Scriptures. But she would say to me each time when I left: "I want so desperately much to go on *living!*"

She must have been a "life actress." I got that impression from the things she told me.

We found her to be a lonely person. She was not married, had almost no family, and remained on her own. Yet she could enjoy life intensely. How was it possible?

As time went on, she suffered more and more pain. The tumor grew in size. Sometimes she was extremely fatigued. She liked being left alone.

We could all see what a difficult time she was having. Putting up a brave front when you know better produces a tremendous tension which becomes unbearable. For me it was clear that she wanted to be reconciled in her private solitude with God.

Even though she didn't talk about things or indicate in any way what was going on inside her, I went into the concerns I believed she must carry within her. Repeatedly I tried to encourage and comfort her. After it was all over I was happy I had been so open with her.

A mere matter of hours before her death she showed how thankful she was for the LORD's continuing care for her. I could read it on her face. This case should make the living all the more convinced of the truth of what we read in Revelation 2:10: "Be faithful until death, and I will give you the crown of life."

Chapter 7

Offering Meaningful Help

*"Therefore whatever you want others to do for you, do
so for them, for this is the Law and the Prophets."*
(Matt. 7:12)

"Be merciful, just as your Father is merciful."
(Luke 6:36)

*"As each one has received a special gift, employ it in
serving one another, as good stewards of the manifold
grace of God."*
(I Pet. 4:10)

Loving service

We have known from earliest childhood what God's law asks of us.
Christ teaches us by way of summary: "'You shall love the Lord your
God with all your heart, and with all your soul, and with all your mind.'
This is the great and foremost commandment. And a second is like it,
'You shall love your neighbor as yourself.' On these two command-
ments depend the whole Law and the Prophets" (Matt. 22:37–40; see
also Heidelberg Catechism, Answer 4).

When we bear this summary in mind, it is clear to us that the love
for our neighbor which God asks of us has nothing in common with the
humanistic solidarity and love of humanity which is so highly praised
nowadays. In fact, these two kinds of love stand diametrically opposed
to one another.

In the case of Humanism, it is not *God* that is central but *man*.
Biblical love for our neighbor, on the other hand, is theocentric. It aims
for the honor of God. It is the fruit of real, operational love for God; it
flows from such love and cannot be understood apart from it. Because
it is like the love we have for God, it does not place the person in need

at the very center; rather, it emphasizes how much we love the LORD and says: *therefore* we love our neighbor. Such love aims to promote our neighbor's well-being as a way to honor the triune God!

If the help we offer, to the sick, the handicapped and the dying is to be meaningful, it must be embedded in an attitude of love that aims at both the horizontal and vertical dimensions of our experience. Therefore our Savior lays down a golden rule for us in Matthew 7:12, where we read: "Therefore whatever you want others to do for you, do so for them, for this is the Law and the Prophets."

This rule is the conclusion of some instruction that precedes it. The Savior sharply condemns a form of lovelessness toward our neighbors that all too often is found among us. We are inclined to magnify the sins and shortcomings of our fellow human beings, while we trivialize our own — the notorious attitude of "the speck and the log" (Matt. 7:3–5). Because we place ourselves on a pedestal and then look down on others, we become guilty of Phariseeism. This is a sin which will not escape God's condemnation.

On the other hand, if we refrain from uttering criticism from on high, this does not mean that we are leaving our neighbor's sinful conduct to run its course. To do so would be just as loveless. The holy things may not be given to the dogs and thereby be defiled (Matt. 7:6). The honor of God is not served if we ignore people's sins. We must let our light shine in this world; we must be gentle and full of love in the way we deal with our neighbors. But at the same time we must act in a responsible way when it comes to the sanctity of God's name.

It is obvious that this attitude of faith calls for a certain amount of self-denial. The Savior has an eye for this realization. He points out that in our varied and often complicated contacts with others, we must use the means God has provided — prayer. Helping hands must at the same time be folded hands.

Of course we also want the good things that come from God's hands for ourselves. And it should go without saying that we want our neighbor to have them as well. Together we are dependent on the mercy of God. In our joint dependence we fulfil, for Christ's sake, the essence of the Law and the Prophets — the great commandment, and a second which is like it.

How great is God's mercy . . .

I hope it is clear to you that the things I affirmed above have to do especially with our contact with those who are in need. Seriously ill patients to whom we minister can react in rather different ways — how they react depends on their situation, their nature, and their degree of understanding. In part because of those differences, it can happen in a given situation that the one offering pastoral help does not know how he must act. In general it can be said that one ought to go about the work with much loving patience and wisdom. One must not come across as distant, but one should not become overly sensitive either.

In this context it is important to pay attention to God's mercy and to let ourselves be led by it. In Luke 6:36 the Savior says, "Be merciful, just as your Father is merciful."

This mercy of God is inexpressibly great. We can never say all there is to be said about it or think it through completely. That He, for our eternal salvation, did not spare His own Son but delivered Him up to death on the cross for our sakes, is something that goes beyond our understanding. That He shows mercy to people like us, people who are ungrateful, people who are evil, people who are His enemies — we just don't understand it. It's all the more mysterious when we consider that we are inclined to repay our neighbor evil for evil.

The mercy of God covers us all of our lives. And we receive it believingly in all the circumstances that can be so painful for us in our flesh. The Scriptures say a great deal about God's incomparable mercy. For Christ's sake He shows this mercy to those who are in misery and need, to those who are alone and sorrowing, to those who are sick and handicapped, to those who are oppressed and downcast, crying out for justice. God's mercy extends to the aged (Ps. 71:9), to those suffering from bodily or mental ailments which cause them to live a life of weariness and pain (Ps. 31), to the weak, to the unfortunate, to those who are dealt with unjustly (Ps. 35). And if you want to know just how great God's mercy is, read Psalm 103. It will make a deep impression on you.

. . . revealed to us in Christ

As I indicated earlier, this love-filled goodness of God is fully revealed in the sending and sacrifice of God's Son, our Lord Jesus Christ. Through what He did for us, He showed that *He* is our merciful High Priest. Therefore He can sympathize with all our weaknesses, for He was tempted in like manner in all things, without Himself falling into sin (Heb. 4:14–16).

In these verses from Hebrews, we read that therefore we can and may go boldly to the throne of grace in order to receive mercy and find grace and be helped in God's time. In this way we can also help others. Christian deeds of mercy are thus to be regarded as a fruit of what Christ has earned on our behalf. They can only be accomplished in living communion with Him!

We must always keep these things in mind if the help we offer is to be meaningful for those we are trying to help. This is all the more the case because those who are in need do not always react in the way that we would wish to see.

Helping others affords us deep satisfaction because it makes us happy in accord with the true meaning of the word happy as we find it in the words of our Savior recorded in Matthew 5:6. Such service is richly blessed. In Matthew 10:42 we read: "And whoever in the name of a disciple gives to one of these little ones even a cup of cold water to drink, truly I say to you he shall not lose his reward."

In this context it is important to bear in mind what the Savior reveals in Matthew 25:31–46 about deeds of mercy having a high priority in God's eyes. Your deeds of mercy will turn out to be an important point in terms of how you are dealt with on the day of judgment. Who are the people who are blessed of the Father and inherit the Kingdom? They are the ones who gave food and drink to the hungry and thirsty Son of man, the ones who took Him in when He was a stranger, who wanted to clothe Him when He was naked, who visited Him when He was sick and in prison.

How are we to regard all these things? Well, says the Savior, by showing mercy to My *brothers*, you have shown it to *Me*. We do this by offering loving service to those about whom the Son and the Father —

our Father — care so deeply. Those who are "least" in the eyes of men are "the greatest" in the eyes of God.

Be merciful, as your Father is merciful. It is within the power of all of us to offer someone a cup of cold water. We don't have to go through a lot of trouble: the water is ready to hand. As for us, we know that we may drink for free from the spring of Life. Let us then, in turn, show compassion to others!

Respect for those who care for the ill

If you have daily experience with the activities in a medical center, you will sense at once how important it is to show respect for those who work there. The people who care for the ill are worth their weight in gold: it is hard to overestimate all that they accomplish during their working hours.

Not only is their work many-sided and exciting, it is also very difficult. It requires them to draw on their entire personality and all their strength. Those who offer such help are responsible for offering good and effective care to patients who react to the situation in which their illness or affliction has placed them. This means that there are many different reactions among the patients, and many of those reactions are influenced in a negative direction by the nature and course of the illness in question. In particular, those who have afflictions of both body and spirit are inclined to create difficulties for the people who take care of them. Even if, in many cases, they cannot help acting the way they do, they still make it hard for the people who look after them.

If you are to go about your work in such a way that you are genuinely useful to the patient, you will need substantial doses of knowledge of people, of patience, of gentleness, and of sheer perseverance. Even then there could be a situation that winds up very unsatisfying and disappointing to you. Many times I have said to someone who was studying to become a worker in the health field, "You will not make it if you do not remember constantly that you are fully dependent on God's mercy."

On the other hand, I have met relatively few people working with the terminally ill who are weighed down by their work all the time. On the contrary, it has often struck me that such people are usually warm and open toward their fellow human beings who need help, that they manifest a great deal of dedication in their work, and that they speak lovingly of "our people."

Of course they admit, if you take the trouble to ask them, that they do not always have such an easy time of it. This stands to reason. It is quite something to spend your working hours in an environment in which the sufferings of this present age are before you large as life, an environment in which you are constantly confronted with the pain that accompanies the final separation here on earth.

Such things do not leave younger people unaffected. But such people admit that they are happy with the appreciation that is shown for their work. It gives them satisfaction to note that patients who are in their charge are willing to entrust themselves fully to their care.

Indeed, it is often refreshing to see what a tight bond there can be between those who are sick and those who are well, between the aged and the young. The realization of this bond brings you pleasure: it activates you and motivates you. It is a privilege to be an instrument in God's hand and to be a channel of His fatherly concern for others.

Those who are aware that they may serve as God's channels feel that they themselves are addressed when Scripture says: "As each one has received a special gift, employ it in serving one another, as good stewards of the manifold grace of God." Yes, the gift of God's grace makes us happy and leaves us feeling rich!

They're not all the same — always . . .

I still remember this sober and wise observation. It was the conclusion of a conversation I had with a somewhat older woman who cared for the sick. Our conversation took place not long after I had begun my work as a minister among the sick. As part of my orientation to the work, I wanted to talk with her in general about her experiences in a social setting in which younger and older people, both healthy and sick, were so closely drawn together.

From the examples passed on to me, it became apparent that the observation I reported above is a striking indication of what actually goes on in a community of living and working together such as one finds in a nursing home. And in the course of the years that followed, I was often to see this observation confirmed.

It is certainly a mark of sober thought to realize that the one person is not the same as the other. Indeed, a person changes over time and cannot be said to be the same always. How varying are the dispositions, reactions, ambitions, and patterns of conduct.

This applies especially to people who find themselves in circumstances in which their pattern of living is influenced by factors that are new to them. Patients and the people who look after them have to get used to such situations and to each other. There are some who never manage it. It should not surprise anyone that tensions spring up. There can be problems and frictions that lead to misunderstandings and to unpleasantness in relationships.

There is always work for us to do in this area, bearing in mind what was said about God's mercy and its fruit in our lives. Permit to illustrate this point from actual practice.

She was thankful and content

It had finally come this far: Mother was brought to our nursing home by two of her adult children. From the conversation I had with the two of them that same day, it was clear to me how difficult it had been to reach this decision. To turn Mother over to strangers far from her trusted and pleasant familiar circle of family and friends — no one wanted to do such a thing to her. They had discussed the matter with her many times. Finally Mother had cut through the knot herself, and now they hoped that she would feel at home in these new surroundings.

As far as I could ascertain, this was never a problem. Mother conducted herself as the person she really was — believing, friendly, thankful, content. And that was how she remained even when she underwent more and more pain and her strength diminished visibly. What patience and joy radiated from her! When I was amazed at this, she said spontaneously, "I do not have all this of myself. The LORD is good to me. In everything that these dear people do for me and around me, I experience His loving faithfulness."

It should surprise no one that such a person was adored in our nursing home. The nurses all wanted the privilege of taking care of her. And her children? They took turns, and a couple of times each week there was someone to visit Mother. It was a pleasure to see how they were united afterward in their thinking. God's ways sometimes seem unfathomable — because that's just what they really are. But they lead, without fail, to the goal He has in mind, a goal that includes the well-being of His children.

They could thank Him for His goodness from the bottom of their hearts. And when Mother died, she was missed not just by her family but by all the people who had helped care for her in the nursing home!

They have written me off

He was a difficult man: almost all the people who dealt with him were agreed on this. He was not very talkative, and he was hard to handle. As one who was severely handicapped, he was surrounded with a lot of love and concern, yet he would *not* cooperate. There were moments when he did the exact opposite of what was asked and expected. And he complained loudly about everything. He maintained that when he was being washed and clothed, people deliberately caused him pain. Often he grumbled about the food. He never had a good word to say about the doctor, and he quarreled constantly with the other patients. The members of the nursing staff were afraid of him.

It was not long before he demanded a room to himself. Once he had it, he became very withdrawn and almost never appeared in the common room, where it was too noisy to suit him. He preferred to eat his meals alone in his room. And to be honest about it, there was no one who missed him at mealtimes. And so he became more and more alone and ever harder to deal with.

Naturally, we realized that something would have to be done. This brother was in need of help. The question was how best to get at him. It seemed that no matter what you said to him, it didn't work. Either he would not respond, or he became angry.

Of course I regarded it as my duty to visit him regularly. But I dreaded the visits. Often my efforts to make contact with him were in vain. On many an occasion he refused to see me and if I did get in, I might not get through to him.

I wanted to know what motivated this man to take such an attitude of discontent. At the weekly meetings I was asked to try and find out the reason for his attitude.

And I succeeded! After working with him for months, I discovered that what I had suspected was indeed the truth of the matter.

The opening in the heart of this brother came almost unexpectedly. The man in the room next to his had died suddenly. He heard about it, and it seemed to affect him. We talked about it. Suddenly he said, "They have written me off too."

When I asked what he meant by this, he began to weep. For a long time he was silent. Neither one of us said anything. I was having a very hard time of it, because I cannot stand to see a man cry. Nevertheless, I repeated my question, and the answer came out in fits and starts. It seems that this brother had been brought to the nursing home with the idea eating away at him that he had been written off by his family and friends. They had all abandoned him and sent him off to a place of death. It would have been better if they had brought him directly to the cemetery.

After this small beginning, his heart began to open up to me further and further. The Spirit used our conversations about the Bible to bring about the reversal for which we had hoped. It is wonderful to see what such a conversion entails.

The proofs of God's mercy now became visible and tangible. The entire section of the nursing home in which he was kept became more lively. In all respects, things were going well. The communion with

God and his neighbor which had been blocked was now restored. In both vertical and horizontal respects, the blocked channels of communication were opened. And in the time that still remained to him, there was a lot of two-way communication.

Of course there was a lot of catching up to do. But it was not difficult, for we all cooperated. How happy he was!

In this case we saw again that the LORD is good. Even though this brother had originally written himself off (without realizing that he had done so), he came to the joyful recognition that he had *not* been written off by God and his fellow human beings. To use his own words, he was a burning brand plucked from the fire.

Chapter 8

Pastoral Care

> "... casting all your anxiety upon Him, because He cares for you." (I Pet. 5:7)

> "I am the good shepherd: and I know My own, and My own know Me, even as the Father knows Me and I know the Father; and I lay down My life for the sheep." (John 10:4–5)

> "... He Himself has said, 'I WILL NEVER DESERT YOU, NOR WILL I EVER FORSAKE YOU,' so that we confidently say, 'THE LORD IS MY HELPER, I WILL NOT BE AFRAID. WHAT SHALL MAN DO TO ME?'" (Heb. 13:5–6)

Caring for the sick is pastoral work

As I indicated earlier, we must not limit the notion of pastoral care to the work done by a minister or an elder or a chaplain. There are more people around a sickbed who are busy in pastoral respects, even if they do not encounter the sick person every day. In fact, every believer who is involved in caring for the sick is engaged in pastoral activity — that is to say, if he or she goes about the work properly.

Some seriously ill people can be cared for at home as terminal patients. It is striking how they can be helped in all sorts of ways by the members of the household as they are surrounded by loving concern. Many may become involved in the project of making the last phase of life as bearable as possible for them. There may be still more people who stand ready to become involved in such care, even though not all would contribute to the same extent.

Naturally, the immediate family comes first. And then, of course, we think of the doctor and the minister. But there are also neighbors, good friends, and sisters of the congregation. An appeal for help made to the latter will usually not go unheeded. It has struck me especially in my own work how much valuable assistance comes from these sisters of the congregation. I have been heartened and encouraged by it.

I'm sure it will not surprise you to hear that I was long intrigued by the question of what motivates such volunteers. What drives them on to perform such selfless service?

I have put this question to a number of them. In most cases I received an answer that made me thankful. What I had hoped to hear was confirmed in what they said. It became apparent that I was not exaggerating when I wrote those words of commendation above.

Christian care for the sick, in its various facets, is indeed pastoral work. When we help our needy neighbor in the way the Bible asks of us, we should be motivated by a desire to follow the Good Shepherd, the one who lays down His life for His sheep. When we consider the burdens and responsibilities we have to shoulder at times, we should remember what the apostle Peter said: we may cast our cares on Him, for He cares for us (I Pet. 5:7).

In this context I also think of what the Savior reveals in John 10:14–15. In this passage He explains that he is the Good Shepherd. Between Him and His sheep there is an intimate bond, a living communion. He knows His sheep and loves them deeply. Therefore He knows exactly what they need and what He must give them.

Moreover, the sheep know Him and show Him their straightforward love. Thus they know to whom they can turn with their needs and cares. And they actually do it!

The Savior compares this acquaintance with the knowledge which the Father and the Son have of one another. Thus the bond could not be any closer.

What is the basis of the reciprocal love between the Good Shepherd and His sheep? The answer is that the Good Shepherd sacrificed His life for them.

Care for the ill that is grounded in the Bible thus flows from what *Christ* has done — and continues to do — for His own. It is a fruit of

Christ's work and sacrifice. Looking to the Good Shepherd and His tender care, the Christian who cares for the sick must know himself to be driven by the desire to show something of that loving care to his neighbors — and then especially to those who have special needs because they are on their deathbed.

Driven by this same spirit of Christ, all who are involved in caring for the ill may see their loving care combined if they are of one heart and mind, so that they are all working toward the same goal — the best possible support for dying patients. They need that care, and because of what Christ has done for them, they deserve it!

Pastoral cooperation is indispensable

We saw earlier how important and necessary it is that there be pastoral cooperation between the family, the minister, the elders of the church, the doctor, and the others who are on the scene to offer assistance. Indeed, cooperation is indispensable. Regular consultation and the exchange of ideas and experiences are strongly recommended. In my many years of experience I have found such exchanges to be most instructive. And it is my impression that the people I was working with appreciated them as much as I did.

This cooperation is ideal if the people who are working together are able to recognize each other as Christians who are all trying to do their work in accordance with God's Word. They will not get in each other's way: they know their own respective tasks and will stay within the proper bounds. They will not work at cross purposes or meddle with each other's responsibilities; instead they will complement each other. No one will pretend that he knows everything there is to know about the situation or that he alone has the power to make decisions.

They will be well aware that they are working toward the same goal — looking after the man or woman who, at the end of life, does not appeal in vain to the Good Shepherd. This is pastoral work at its very best!

In one of our papers a while ago, I read an article by Mr. A. P. Wisse, which appealed to me. In some previous articles he had written about the hospices in England which are used more and more to care for people who are dying. There are about a hundred of these institutions there. Most of them are Roman Catholic or Anglican in orientation. They take in terminal patients who have been discharged from hospitals in order to care for them during their last weeks or months. The kind of care they offer is not possible within a hospital setting. Most of the patients in a hospice are suffering from the final stages of cancer.

Mr. Wisse talked with J. F. Hanratty, the medical director of the St. Joseph's Hospice in London. According to Wisse, the hospice movement in England may provide a partial answer to the questions being raised in the Netherlands concerning euthanasia. Right now there are about 6000 cases of euthanasia per year in the Netherlands; that number could be greatly reduced if a system of hospices were established here.

A hospice is a small nursing facility established to care for people who are dying. Good efforts are made to combat the pain they are suffering. They are taught to accept the situation in which they find themselves, so that manifestations of stress can be eliminated as much as possible.

In the article I read, Mr. Wisse went into the question to what extent Reformed hospices are necessary and feasible. He had put this question to Dr. E. S. Oosterhuis, medical director of a Reformed center for nursing and reactivation in the Netherlands. Dr. Oosterhuis pointed out that setting up such hospices would be far from easy. In any case, the terminal patients must be given all-around care. In more than one instance, professional help has proven to be necessary — the kind of help that can only be given in a responsible way in a facility where there are nurses.

Dr. Oosterhuis was in favor of trying to establish support centers in every province of the Netherlands, centers which would be equipped with all the facilities needed to look after terminal patients. But because of all the efforts to keep medical costs in line, it did not appear likely to him that such centers would soon come into existence.

In passing on the thinking of Dr. Oosterhuis, Wisse did not mean to suggest that the hospice idea should not draw the interest of Reformed people. Rather, he pleaded for an effort to take hold of any possibility that presents itself so that when members of our churches face death, they can be as close as possible to the circles of their family members and fellow believers. He also pointed out that our population is growing older, and so we can expect to have more dying people in our midst. Moreover, the danger of euthanasia is much greater now than it used to be — not only in hospitals but also in nursing facilities. These are certainly words that are worth considering carefully!

Wisse is especially interested in what church members do to care for each other and meet each other's needs. Such care should of course be present at an optimal level in times of good health, but we must also consider times of sickness and the approach of death. The special provisions connected with such situations may change, but the task and obligation remains the same.

Thus there cannot be any question whether pastoral cooperation is necessary. But it is indeed a question whether it is always possible to provide it.

It almost took my breath away

It is not hard to see that those who work with terminal patients must be spiritually equipped for their task. They need to increase their Bible knowledge through regular study of the Scriptures. This is an important point.

The special character of their work shows that Bible knowledge is indispensable if they are to be able to think through and discuss and solve the kinds of problems they encounter.

What happens in practice is that some medical person who establishes a good relationship with a patient comes to be trusted by that patient and is then told certain things in confidence. In such a setting there may arise some questions and difficulties that have to do with the patient's experience of his or her faith. A helping hand then has to be offered. This applies to both nurses and their aides as well as doctors.

This is not to say that these medical personnel have to carry a Bible with them on their rounds. In any case, they generally do not have time for long conversations and need to restrict themselves to their medical duties. That's why it is important for such people to have good contact with the pastor: the patients will benefit from good working relations.

In this connection I think back with gratitude to a time when I was working in our nursing center. On a weekly basis we had consultations between the doctors and the pastor. These well-attended "team meetings" were worthwhile and instructive: they met a need. Because of the cooperation that had been established in this way, it sometimes happened late at night that a doctor or nurse would offer spiritual support to a dying person while the pastor, who had just been contacted by telephone, was on his way. In such situations, doctors and nurses exercised their task as priests.

When I entered the room of the dying patient, it was moving for me to see how well the nurse on duty was handling the situation. She had read some Bible verses aloud, and I could begin my work by appealing to those verses. It almost took my breath away!

Many-sided pastoral care

A pastor who takes the welfare of his sheep to heart feels obliged to work for the spiritual well-being of the whole congregation. Therefore his work of sermon preparation will be paired with regular contact with those who have extra needs. Here I think especially of the sick, the aged, the lonely, the handicapped, those who have suffered a serious loss, and those who are inclined to keep to themselves.

A pastor who makes such cares his special concern will notice how much his own example stimulates and motivates people. And when he appeals for help to others who are also busy with pastoral matters, it will not be in vain.

The same comments could be made about those who work together within a nursing facility. The pastor would do well to organize and even lead various activities designed to equip the people in the facilities for the challenges they face. He must deal with patients who are chronically ill, patients who for the most part sense that they will never be able to go home again, patients who have difficulty dealing with others in the strange environment in which they find themselves or who are upset at sudden, unexpected deaths. Moreover, he also shares in the care given to a good number of psycho-geriatric patients — older people who are orally handicapped or suffer from some mental dementia.

To help them in a way that is effective, it may be advisable to involve them in group discussions in addition to the one-on-one visits they receive. Such group sessions should be set up in consultation with the doctors, department heads, and nursing personnel.

Among those with physical ailments, regular Bible study groups can be established. In these sessions, passages of Scripture and parts of the Reformed confessions are discussed. There can also be some "free topics" brought forward by the participants themselves. It has struck me repeatedly how eager these patients are to be fully a part of everyday life.

They want to experience and discuss the things that go on in our country and our world today. They don't want to be parked at the side of the road or placed on a side track. They don't like to be shoved into a special little corner for sick people.

Do you know what interests them in particular? An open exchange of ideas about such topics as euthanasia, suicide, life and death, the assurance of faith, responsible prayer, God's response to our prayers, election in relation to the covenant, burial, and cremation.

On the other hand, psycho-geriatric patients are not always open to such discussions. Some of them can hardly be reached, for they express themselves only with great difficulty, or perhaps not at all. It is my experience that some of them are more likely to open up in a group setting involving the people who are around them every day than in a one-on-one situation.

The pastor who visits them must therefore know how to enlist others in the effort to reach such people. I would recommend bringing such a group together a couple of times per week in a quiet place. A short Bible story can then be told in a simple way. Singing also has its place: when the pastor sings beloved psalms and hymns, the effect can be amazing, even if no one else joins in. I have succeeded a number of times in first getting through to someone through singing. We can rest assured that the LORD loves to hear us sing!

But what we should remember especially is that through this kind of help, which is often so hard to offer, *He* shows how tenderly He cares for such children. After all, He did promise them at the beginning of their lives: "I will never desert you, nor will I ever forsake you" (Heb. 13:5).

On this basis we can rest assured that He *continues* to help His children, however weak or passive they may have become in mental respects. He will lead them right to the day of their death!

To be assured of his presence right from the cradle to the grave is surely the finest certainty a human being could hope to possess. There is no illegible "fine print" in the insurance policy we call the gospel. Every page is clearly readable. The gospel has an eternal value for every person who has received it from God and thus has made it his own.

There is much more I could say about the many facets of pastoral work. But what I have said will, I trust, give you a solid impression of it. I will conclude my consideration of this subject with a few instructive episodes that speak for themselves.

Mother is at the point of death

As I was making my preparations that Sunday, the telephone rang. The woman's voice I heard when I answered was not familiar to me. She asked me politely, but with a note of urgency. "Could you come right away? Mother is at the point of death."

When I asked who "Mother" was, I was given a name and address. Neither was familiar to me. But where there is a need there must be no delay. I set out at once.

The reception I got was revealing. The daughter could hardly believe her eyes when she saw me standing before her already. "Wonderful — you see, you are an 'Article 31' minister, and we're just plain Reformed, but that makes no difference. Better someone than no one. You should know that our own minister has left us on our own for a couple of years already. You never see him at our place. Mother doesn't like him — he's too liberal in his thinking. That's why she wanted me to call you. On your deathbed you would like to hear that Jesus really existed and that there really is a heaven — right?" I could not deny it. But before I went to the mother's room, the daughter assured me, "If you get on well with her, you may also conduct the funeral."

And that's how it turned out: I did conduct the funeral. But it didn't happen right away. It turned out that Mother was not at the point of death that day when I was asked to come. Mother and I had a few weeks together, and, I must add, I enjoyed the time we had. She was a woman from the old school, shall we say, and did not feel "at home" in her church any more — in fact, she had not felt at home there for many years. "They give us stones for bread," she said, "since our leaders think they have discovered that God's Word is a purely human document that stems from ancient times." Back in the 1940s, her husband had chosen not to "go with Schilder." She explained: "After all, you don't leave the church for the sake of one man — don't you agree?"

There was no point in getting into an argument about this matter. It seemed best to me to emphasize that the Gospel is always reliable since it was not made up by human beings. In her case, too, it showed itself to be the power of God unto salvation.

Mother heard familiar sounds and responded to them with joy. The things I said to her were also the things she had learned and affirmed years before.

To make a long story short, the Word did its work in her case. Mother fell asleep peacefully and was buried in the Christian manner. The daughter was seen attending "our services." At first it was only now and then. Was she perhaps trying to repay us? But no, that's not what she was doing. God's Word was also doing its work in her. Now, for some years, she has been a member of our local church — the one that remained Reformed. She joined on her own, and with great pleasure.

A hellish spectacle around the casket

It happened during my period in Brazil. About nine o'clock in the evening, a Brazilian knocked on my back door. The man asked whether I would bring him, in my jeep, to a town some twelve kilometers down the road. A young, unmarried mother and her baby had just died. I agreed to bring him to the scene.

When we arrived at the home where the deaths had taken place, I could hardly believe my eyes and ears. In and around the house were hundreds of Brazilians, old and young. They were singing, screaming, and clapping their hands. In this manner they were trying to chase the evil spirits away, or at least keep them at a distance. What a frightful spectacle surrounding the casket!

Now, the "casket" consisted of a pair of rough planks on a support base. On the planks were some spotless white sheets. On these sheets lay the mother and her baby, next to each other, motionless, surrounded by flowers and burning grease-pots. It was a stunning sight.

I stayed there for hours, with all the people staring at me. I was the only white person in a sea of brown faces.

It was well past midnight when I finally asked for silence. I opened my Portuguese Bible and read aloud from Romans 8:31–39. There was silence: the people were listening. They also listened to the words I spoke to them in their national language, even though my command of their language left something to be desired.

I pointed to the necessity of believing in Christ, the only Mediator between God and man. Christ gave Himself up in death for all who believe in Him. Those who realize this will no longer be afraid of evil spirits. The devil and his henchmen flee before Christ, who conquered death.

After I left, the spectacle started up anew. During the ride back home (morning light was breaking by this time), I pondered some encouraging words: although man sows in weakness, the Lord sees to the harvest. The living Word is much more powerful than the meaningless noise generated by people. The devils know this — and tremble!

Let me enjoy it for just one hour more

She was an artistically-inclined woman. She loved nature and could walk for hours in the woods. She was enchanted by fresh green growth in springtime and the beautiful display of colors that break out each fall.

As a teacher in one of our schools, she knew how to make students enthusiastic about God's beautiful creation. She talked about the creation in a sensitive way: you could not help but be struck by it. She often said to me, "And then, just think — all this is only a paltry beginning of the eternal joy that awaits us.

"It will really be something to be with all the redeemed when we have direct contact with the Triune God in the renewed cosmos. It is unimaginable how wonderful it will be to enjoy ourselves in all that God has created once it has been freed for good from His curse. What a wonderful prospect!"

What she confessed here so freely she also experienced to the full, even in the period when she could no longer stand up and go where she wanted. She knew she was ill and that the doctors had no remedies for her. She had it figured out even before she was told officially.

In this period, too, she sought her strength and courage in the LORD. Not once in those final days was she put to shame in this regard, however difficult things became for her.

Right to the end, it was possible for her to be cared for at home. Her bed was by the window, which afforded her a view of the park, with some trees in the background. For the last time, she enjoyed the changing seasons, each with its special charm. During times when she was feeling reasonably well, her enjoyment was plain to see.

Then fall came. Most of the time it was rainy weather, and there was considerable wind. But now and then we had a bright day with plenty of sunshine.

On one of the bright days she said to me, "How I would love to go out in those woods once more for an hour to enjoy the parade of colors. Just look — what overwhelming beauty!"

An idea came to me at once, but I did not tell her what I had in mind. First I would have to talk with the doctor, the nurse who stopped in regularly to attend to her, and the family members. They all agreed that on a day when she felt fairly well, I should take her on a ride through the woods in my automobile.

A suitable day soon arrived. It was glorious weather — not much wind, plenty of sun. You couldn't ask for a better day. When I asked her that morning, "Would you like to come with me this afternoon for a ride through the woods?" she couldn't believe her ears. It had become a reality. My wife and the nurse came along. The patient sat in the front seat, warmly dressed and supported by cushions. However long I live, I will never forget that journey.

Her eyes, usually so dull, beamed with joy. It was almost too much for them to take it all in. Although her voice was weak by that point, we heard repeated sounds of pleasure from her. She couldn't get enough of it: the hour's ride was over too soon.

When we brought her back home, she was very tired but content. In the striking language that was typical of her, she said, "How beautiful it was! If this is what the outer porches look like, just imagine how beautiful the great halls must be!" A week later she was able to see those great halls for herself!

Chapter 9

Faithful Until Death

"If we confess our sins, He is faithful and righteous to forgive us our sins and to cleanse us from all unrighteousness."   (I John 1:9)

"The LORD will accomplish what concerns me; Thy lovingkindness, O LORD, is everlasting; do not forsake the works of Thy hands."   (Ps. 138:8)

"Let us hold fast the confession of our hope without wavering, for He who promised is faithful."
(Heb. 10:23)

"Be faithful until death, and I will give you the crown of life."   (Rev. 2:10)

Faithfulness must be evident

In my conversations with young people, I like to raise questions that arise from the practice of life. One of the questions I ask is whether we can always be sure of our eternal salvation.

Usually this question is met with silence — a remarkable silence. People don't know where to go with the question. Even less do they dare give a positive answer to it. As the conversation progresses, it soon becomes apparent where the shoe pinches.

Isn't it possible for all sorts of things to happen to a believer before he dies? He can fall into sin, and even remain mired in sin. Many examples could be given.

Of course, on the day you made public profession of your faith, you promised that you would obey the LORD and would persevere in this commitment. But did you, at that moment, clearly foresee the con-

97

sequences of such a commitment? Surely that was impossible! And yet, you are supposed to remain faithful — all through your life!

But look around you for a moment. It is not to be denied that in our churches we see more and more cases of discipline, excommunication, and people leaving the church. Moreover, young people are often disappointed in the conduct of the older people, who presumably possess a lot more Bible knowledge and therefore should be steadier on their spiritual feet, so to speak.

And so it seems wise to me to raise the question openly with young people. I bring it up when I see an opening. And it is a fact that many an elderly person or seriously ill person has difficulty with this question. Here we see the value of learning the important lessons when we are still young.

Believing permanently

It is true that faithfulness must be evident — not just once but again and again. It is also true that not everyone perseveres in this regard — far from it. Not even all who once made a public promise to be faithful manage to persevere. But to make these points is not yet to have shown that you cannot be sure of your eternal salvation. What is the real question here?

A believer who pledges to be faithful to God remains bound to his word for God's sake. That's precisely why he must believe *permanently*. He must always be busy with his faith as a gift received from God.

The LORD does not give more faith to the one person than to the other. The quantity is the same in each case, and so is the quality. We cannot speak in terms of more faith and less faith.

The Savior rejects any talk of increasing one's faith. His disciples had asked Him for exactly this, but He pointed out to them that they were to draw strength from their faith — the strength God had given them in and through their faith (Luke 17:5–6).

Peter fell short in this regard. That's why he almost drowned in the turbulent waters of the Sea of Galilee and came to be called a man of "little faith" by the Savior (Matt. 14:30–31).

In contrast, the Canaanite woman continued to exercise her faith after the disappointment of not seeing her original request granted. From the mouth of the Savior she heard: "O woman, your faith is great; be it done for you as you wish" (Matt. 15:28).

There is nothing within ourselves that gives us the guarantee that we will be able to persevere in our faith. It is not in our own strength that we can always show ourselves to be faithful and reach the intended goal when the period of struggle — our life — comes to an end. It is only in the power of Christ that we can be assured that we will indeed reach the finish line, for He is our highest Leader and the Finisher of our faith. If we cling to Him in all circumstances, we are assured that when we draw our final breath, no one and nothing will be able to separate us from His love.

It is true that we sin much and often. We do not always show ourselves to be faithful in the manner which the LORD asks of us. The first thing we must do is confess this simply and not take refuge in any talk to the effect that we don't know how to be faithful or don't have the strength to do so. That way we will be even closer to Christ and find refuge in Him all the more. Only then will things go well with us and come out as they should. Remember the assurance we read in Scripture: "If we confess our sins, He is faithful and righteous to forgive us our sins and to cleanse us from all unrighteousness" (I John 1:9).

Living in the assurance of eternal life, now and always, means living in the forgiving grace of God, for Christ's sake. When we follow this path, we need not doubt our eternal salvation for even a moment. As proof of this truth, we have a great crowd of "crown witnesses" around us. We can read about them in Hebrews 11.

The LORD is as faithful as He is strong

God's faithfulness toward us and our children can rightly be compared to His strength. Both are unlimited and immeasurable. Both go beyond our understanding.

Where do we see the faithfulness of the LORD revealed? In His covenant with us — with younger ones and older ones. He made this covenant with us in His sovereign good pleasure. And He does not let go of the works of His hands; He will finish what He started.

Thus, despite all the unfaithfulness that we see in our own life and in the lives of others, we know that when we appeal to His mercy, it will not be in vain. There is no end to His mercy (Ps. 138:8).

How do we come to this realization? Practice shows that people who are seriously ill and those who are dying may come into a crisis situation. Now, without repeating what I have already written about such matters, let me draw your attention once again to a single point.

In a phase of dying that may last for a shorter or longer period, believers can sometimes encounter great spiritual difficulties — especially those who wavered somewhat during their lives and never knew much of the assurance of faith. Others begin to doubt when they think back over the course of their life and ponder the many sins and failures they find there. Still others face temptations with regard to matters that used to cause them no difficulties. And then there are some who dread the prospect of dying because they know that afterward will come the great encounter with God.

To offer pastoral assistance in cases like these means that we must not only be very careful but also be resolute and determined. What every believer, in the years when he is healthy, must learn to know and begin to draw on is the very thing he must now hold before himself when he is on his deathbed, namely, God's unshaken faithfulness. God knows — more fully than we ever realize — just how lacking in courage and weak in physical strength we are. The One who repeatedly picked us up and kept us on the right track showed thereby how much we mean to Him. Will He not also make this apparent when we come to the end of our days? Remember that He promised to do exactly that! He has not taken back the assurance He gave us: "Whether we live or die, we are the Lord's" (Rom. 14:8).

In some published death announcements we read: "He has passed on in the hope of eternal life." Such an expression should not be taken as including an element of doubt, as all too often seems to be the case.

We should not read such an announcement as drawing a contrast between hoping, on the one hand, and knowing with certainty, on the other.

No, what this testimony should really make us think of is the Christian hope that is *certain* of what has been promised. Such is the confession to which we must cling unshaken — even when the hour of death approaches. We are able to do this because "He who promised is faithful" (Heb. 10:23).

Our faithfulness, which is grounded in God's faithfulness and flows from it, is richly rewarded. We can rest assured that He will reward us in His grace. The "crown of life" which is promised us (Rev. 2:10) means that we will get a royal reception in the kingdom of heaven.

When we offer pastoral help that incorporates these Scriptural assurances, we invigorate the people to whom we minister. God's blessing then is sure!

Ready for the great encounter

He was a strong man. That he was spiritually strong is easy to understand. And it was the reason why a number of people in the congregation to which he belonged did not like him. They found him too self-assured. He did not "look within" often enough to suit them. Thereby he was lacking — so they thought — in knowledge of our sin and misery. You see, if you only sense how worthy of condemnation you really are in God's sight, you talk a different way. Then you do not go on and on about the unshakable covenant and the certainty of God's promises. For the question is then whether those promises are *for you personally*. After all, the corrupt heart of man can so easily mislead us. What human being — worthy of eternal condemnation — dares to assert that he has been chosen for eternal life?

Our brother did not feel very much at home in the congregation either. During his very first visit to the men's society, he got into something of a confrontation with some of the brothers. And the situation did not improve at subsequent meetings. People called him "the covenant man" and suggested that he was not sufficiently serious about sin and salvation.

On one occasion he was asked specifically whether he could be sure, right then and there, of his eternal salvation. Without any hesitation he answered with a yes. Then he went on to explain. He pointed out that subjective feelings within us are not decisive when it comes to such a matter — the reliable Word of God is what counts. Whoever clings to that Word in faith is ready for the great encounter at any moment. After all, the LORD will keep the promise He made at the time of baptism. He does so by making us willing and ready to live for him.

It became quite a discussion. Bible texts poured down like rain, as those who did not agree with him tried to drive him into a corner. He was reminded that it is written that those who cry out "Lord, Lord" will be disappointed. Indeed, it is hardly possible for a righteous person to be saved. And isn't it also true that we can often be a disappointment to ourselves and to others? Our intentions may be good and we may take the right steps, but what really counts is our *deeds*. All too often, they are in conflict with what we set out to do. And when the day of judgment comes, the LORD will judge each one on the basis of his works!

Our brother listened to all of this talk patiently. But he did not feel overwhelmed. He responded, "If it indeed depended on us, we would be eternally lost, for we are sinful people. What the apostle Paul writes is true: 'For I know that nothing good dwells in me, that is, in my flesh; for the wishing is present in me, but the doing of the good is not' (Rom. 7:18)." He continued by saying, "I would also point to the conclusion in verse 21. There I find the principle that when I wish to do good, evil is present in me." He explained further that this was why he heartily endorsed what the apostle says in the verses 24 and 25: "Wretched man that I am! Who will set me free from the body of this death? Thanks be to God through Jesus Christ our Lord!"

When he told me this story, we found we were one in our hearts, for we both knew: "The fear of the LORD is the beginning of wisdom; a good understanding have all those who do His commandments; His praise endures forever" (Ps. 111:10). Our brother continued to cling to this confession. On his deathbed he declared: "God's grace has been *sufficient* for me all my life long. Therefore I could say before — and I can say it now — that I am ready for the great encounter."

She would not be comforted

The very first time I visited him, I already sensed that I was not really welcome. After I introduced myself, I saw his face fall somewhat. I soon found out the reason. Of course he believed and read the Bible regularly. But he wanted nothing to do with "educated ministers." He found them too artificial; therefore he never went to church. But with his wife he listened to tapes on Sundays. The sermons on the tapes were from some sort of "deep" lay preacher. Before his death, this "lay" preacher had seen to it that his sphere of influence would become even greater. It was amazing how he could preach! He did not undertake any preparation, and he used no notes whatsoever. That was a true minister for you! You were laid bare: you were confronted with what you were. Perhaps, in such a manner, it was still possible to receive a glimmer of hope — but then it had to be given to you.

I finally asked him whether he believed Christ had died for his sins and guaranteed him eternal life. He looked at me in a manner I had encountered before. In his eyes I was someone who took religious matters too lightly.

A number of times I tried to get significant contact with this man. I read short passages from Scripture, which I hoped would lead him from the darkness of his own one-sided thinking to the clear light of deliverance and of the rich life that is ours in Christ. But he didn't understand. Or was it that he *refused* to understand?

His death came unexpectedly. I was asked to inform his wife. She was home when I called on her, and I communicated my news to her carefully. Her reaction was very striking, for she began to cry pitiably. I let her cry, but after about half an hour I tried to help her by pointing out that we do not need to mourn as those who have no hope (I Thess. 4:13).

Her response to my statement amazed me, for she began to cry all the more. As she wailed, she stammered: "I am so afraid that my husband is lost eternally. He was never able to see any light in the darkness. Nor could I."

Whatever I tried to do, this woman would not be comforted. The situation made a deep impression on me as I went my way again. And then I thought back to something my father had said to me on the basis of his own pastoral experience: "My boy, always remember that there are people who think they have been in hell but go to heaven, and vice versa."

Confused, but not helpless

Because of my travels to various parts of the globe, I had not seen her for twenty years. Yet I remembered her very clearly. She was getting on in years when she took steps to join the church, but she had not yet made her profession of faith.

She was going to receive some instruction from me by way of preparation. It was apparent that she possessed the knowledge that was needed. But her spiritual background and the things she had been taught earlier still played a part in her life. She came from a background where it is customary for young people to make their profession without promising that they will go to the Lord's table. Such an attitude is even respected in the circles she came from.

She wanted nothing to do with such double-mindedness. She understood very well that when you answered in the affirmative as you made profession of faith, you were at the same time asking for permission to go to the Lord's table.

Yet she had always had difficulty with the thought of the Lord's table. She still did. From her upbringing it had been hammered into her that you can easily eat and drink judgment to yourself. That background was still active in her thinking.

We did a lot of talking about this matter. Repeatedly I pointed out that Christ's invitation is at the same time a command — and then not one that stands alone but one that is accompanied with an appeal for repentance.

We studied the form for the Lord's supper. We talked especially about the passages dealing with self-examination as we explored what it means to go to the Lord's table. She came to see that we do not go to God's covenant table to demonstrate that we are such upstanding people but only because we desire to seek our life outside of ourselves in Jesus Christ.

Gradually she began to understand and respond. She made profession of her faith. But not one of the members of her family was in church for the occasion. She was hurt by this, but joy was still uppermost. How bravely she sang along with the congregation that Sunday: "Forever I will thank and praise Thee; It is Thy doing, LORD" (Ps. 52, rhymed version).

What happened to her after that I did not know for many years. One day, unexpectedly, I found out. A woman who was a good friend of hers telephoned me. By this point my former catechism pupil was over eighty years of age. Before she died, she wanted to see the man who had instructed her in the faith.

It was a joyous reunion. Again we talked a great deal. Her family had ignored her all those years, and she had passed up many opportunities to involve herself in contacts with the members of the congregation. But her pastor had played an enormous role in her life: what support she had received from him!

She had often needed extra pastoral attention. A number of times she fell back into her "old evil." She had gone through the depths. There were times when she was confused, when she didn't know what to do, believing that God had forsaken her. During such periods she was not able to pray and she stayed away from the Lord's table, with the result that she felt ever more guilty.

She told me that her spiritual background had almost been her undoing. And she came to see how unbiblical this spiritual subjectivism really is.

During one of her crises, her pastor had read Psalm 73 with her. Then she saw it at once: she recognized what a fool she had been. The

LORD, who held her by her right hand, did not let go of her! And now that she would die before long, she was sure of it: "With Thy counsel Thou will guide me, and afterward receive me to glory" (Ps. 73:24).

It was time to say goodbye. I still hear her saying, "I was confused, but not helpless." And I was reminded of the words of Scripture: "Be faithful until death, and I will give you the crown of life" (Rev. 2:10).

Chapter 10

Christian Burial

"For this reason it says, 'AWAKE, SLEEPER, AND ARISE FROM THE DEAD, AND CHRIST WILL SHINE ON YOU.'"
(Eph. 5:14)

"Do not marvel at this; for an hour is coming, in which all who are in the tombs shall hear his voice, and shall come forth . . ."   (John 5:28–29)

"So also is the resurrection of the dead. It is sown a perishable body, but it is raised an imperishable body."   (I Cor. 15:42)

"For the Lord will not reject forever, for if He causes grief, then He will have compassion according to His abundant loving-kindness. For He does not afflict willingly, or grieve the sons of men."
(Lam. 3:31–33)

More than an ordinary ritual

For me it has never been an open question whether our dead should be buried or cremated. It is my conviction that they must receive a Christian burial.

Regular burial is still permitted in the Netherlands, even though land is in short supply. Yet no one knows how long we will continue to possess this freedom. Cremation is becoming ever more common.

It must be burial: in this regard I subscribe in general to what has been said about this matter by Reformed writers. A careful study of the extensive documentation and argumentation on this question seems to me to be more necessary than ever.

No one can deny that Scripture makes it clear that the practice of burying the dead has been with us for many centuries. Because we are one in the faith with the believers in the Bible, it seems to me that we should continue the practice.

What is of greatest significance, in my judgment, is what the Bible says about the burial of Christ and the fruits of that burial. His burial rightly forms an important part of our undoubted Christian faith and is mentioned explicitly in the Apostles Creed.

With regard to God the Son and our redemption, we confess that He suffered, died, *was buried*, and rose from the dead on the third day. These four facts are recited by the church in one breath. They are closely connected to one another. The one fact may not be separated from the others. They form a single golden chain of Christ's work as Mediator. Their connection with one another is also of immeasurable value for us as believers.

What do we learn from Scripture? That the fruit of Christ's work as our Savior (including His burial) is enjoyed in life and death — thus also in our everyday life! The Heidelberg Catechism teaches us: "Through Christ's death our old nature is crucified, put to death, and buried with him, so that the evil desires of the flesh may no longer reign in us, but that we may offer ourselves to Him as a sacrifice of thankfulness" (Answer 43; see also Rom. 6:6, 8, 11–12).

If we don't want the sinful desires of our corrupt heart to dominate us any longer, we must not only declare them dead but must see to it that they go *into the grave* — with Christ. Thereby we respond to the apostolic appeal in Ephesians 5:14: "Awake, sleeper, and arise from the dead, and Christ will shine on you." When it comes to our deathbed, we have to realize that our death is followed by burial, which is in turn bound up inseparably with "the resurrection of the body."

On the basis of His burial and resurrection (note the unity) Christ guarantees us that ". . . an hour is coming, in which all who are in the tombs shall hear his voice, and shall come forth; those who did the good deeds, to a resurrection of life . . ." (John 5:28–29).

What happened in the case of Christ will also happen with those who belong to Him. In the words of the apostle Paul: "So also is the resurrection of the dead. It is sown a perishable body, but it is raised an imperishable body" (I Cor. 15:42). Thus Christ's burial was more than a ritual, more than an observance of a familiar custom of a bygone age. It is a salvation fact that happened for the sake of our redemption!

A social event

Before the second world war, a burial was much more of a social event than it is today. This was true especially in areas where the inhabitants of a village formed a tight community. Almost everyone felt affected when there was a death; all were drawn in. I can recall from my youth how someone, acting on behalf of the family, would go door to door to pass the news that So-and-so had died. This was done in carefully chosen, solemn language. At the same time, this person would invite the people he contacted to attend the funeral.

This practice made an impression on me. The whole village would swing into action, especially if the person who died was well known and loved. The attendance at the burial would usually be substantial. The people in the neighborhood would help the family bear the cost by making financial contributions and also by offering their services. On the first Sunday after the burial, the period of mourning would be reflected in the service as well, and the church would be very full. The mourning went on for weeks.

By way of comparison, the burial ceremonies of more recent years are rather sober and down-to-earth. Many people belong to some sort of funeral or burial society, which looks after everything. There is almost nothing left for the immediate family to do. The arrangements will probably involve a funeral home where the dead body can be viewed. In this establishment, family and friends can be visited at a time set specifically for offering condolences. And it is from this funeral home that the actual burial arrangements are carried out. For people who live in a small house in which there is not enough room to receive a lot of visitors offering condolences — and there are many such people — such arrangements are indeed necessary. And often I have been touched by the dignified, Christian manner in which the funeral director went about his work.

What happens quite often nowadays is that the actual burial is done privately. Only the members of the immediate family and some relatives who are very close to them gather around the grave.

But when this is done, the burial, as an event, is closed off to a number of people who would like to show their interest and concern. Naturally, the wishes of the deceased and/or his family need to be the final word in such a matter. All the same, I would not advise moving in such a direction. It should only be done if there are very convincing reasons.

On the other hand, things do not need to be done just the way they were done in the old days. Yet I would like to see the social aspect of a burial maintained and practiced. Especially in the case of a Christian burial, the social aspect should be respected, so that people who are not part of the immediate family have some opportunity to participate.

Attending a funeral and burial may give rise to feelings that are truly heart-warming. As we give thanks to the LORD, there is still room to say something about what the deceased has meant in the church, at work, and for friends and family. It seems to me a sound practice to take leave of a person who, through God's goodness, was able to play an important role in our midst, provided we do so in a Christian manner.

And such leave-taking can most certainly be pleasing to the LORD — especially if He is thanked for the social settings within which we were able to serve Him throughout our lives. A number of times I have remarked how dignified and God-glorifying such funerals can be. They offer encouragement to the bereaved family and serve as a striking testimony of what the communion of saints means in times of sorrow and disappointment. They enable us to take a step ahead as we work through the grieving process. Christian burials can be rich blessings — also for those who have long stood on the edges of church life.

No scenes at the deathbed

Of course, you think to yourself, "No thoughtful Christian would want scenes at the deathbed." But this doesn't mean that they never occur. What I am writing about here can be painful for many people; yet there are some things that need to be said. It is necessary to protest against certain abuses in homes where death is about to enter. We have to take measures to keep out the things that do not belong there — quarrels involving the children and/or in-laws, disputes about all sorts of things. I think especially of the bickering that can take place when the possessions are to be divided — in case no proper will has been drawn up with the help of a lawyer.

Such disputes are all too common in homes where death has entered. A dying father or mother can be deeply distressed by them. I know of a number of cases in which a dying father or mother cried bitter tears about such disputes.

When it comes to the inheritance, relatives can be very hard on each other and even be brutally insensitive toward the dying person. In some cases, they manage to take away from the Christian character of the burial.

Such disputes can cause great difficulties for the pastor. He knows what is going on and may even have spoken to the adult children about it. He has told them that they must be reconciled with one another. Perhaps he has enlisted the help of the doctor in an effort to convince the trouble-makers that their attitude at the deathbed is irresponsible from a medical point of view as well.

In more than one case, the efforts of a pastor in such circumstances have not succeeded in making things better. On the day of the burial there is great tension to be felt. The adult children who hated and ignored one another sat in the front of the church next to each other, stood around the open grave together, and then sat around the same table at a reception following the burial. And those who knew what was going on realized that once the day of burial was over, the estrangement among them would grow even greater.

There must not be scenes at the deathbed. To engage in such behavior is to commit an offense against one's parents. And it is an abomination in the eyes of the LORD, a sin that He will not leave unpunished.

Not a worship service but an assembly

In a Reformed church order you will find an article to the effect that there are not to be any worship services to mourn the dead. For example, in Article 65 of the Church Order of the Canadian Reformed Churches, we read: "Funerals are not ecclesiastical but family affairs, and should be conducted accordingly."

Thus the assembly we hold before we go to the cemetery is not to be regarded as one of the church's worship services. Nothing should be done to create the impression that it is a worship service. The person who leads the service (usually a minister) does not do so in the name of the consistory. No elder conducts him to the front of the church and shakes his hand before he goes to the pulpit. There is no votum and greeting at the beginning, nor do the assembled people receive the LORD's blessing at the end.

It is at the family's request that he leads the service. In my judgment, there is therefore no reason why one should not conduct a funeral at the request of people who do not belong to your own fellowship of churches or to a sister church, provided it is understood in advance that there will be no restriction on the proclamation of the Gospel and also that the funeral will not be passed off as some sort of ecclesiastical worship service.

In such a service the Word of God must be central. The passages of Scripture to be read and the psalms and hymns to be sung must all be chosen with an eye to the situation.

The same applies to the prayers. The God of all grace and comfort wants to proceed with His work and wants His Word to be heard. A funeral service should be short and should be marked by sobriety and honesty.

What a rich blessing such a service can be! More than once in my ministry I was able to take up contact with people previously unknown to me because they were family members or friends of someone whose funeral I had conducted. A Christian burial apparently makes an impression on such people.

In such simple services as funerals, the Holy Spirit is at work too. The Word of life causes new birth and gives genuine life, even in painful circumstances when we are confronted with death and the grave!

Around the open grave — and afterwards

Everything that happens in the short funeral service ought to be directed toward lifting up our hearts to Christ, who proclaims Himself to be the Life and has made life triumph over death. In the strength of this conviction of faith, we unite ourselves with the family as we stand around the open grave.

We must then confess honestly that if it were not for the LORD's special care for us, we would have been overpowered by pain. We sense this especially at the moment when we look into that deep, dark opening as the casket is let down.

I have been asked on occasion which I prefer — leaving the casket above ground or having it lowered while the people are still in attendance. My advice is to choose the latter. As long as the casket is above ground, *burial* has not really taken place!

Of course I am well aware of the special pains and sorrows that may strike people at the exact moment when the casket is lowered slowly but surely into the grave. At that critical juncture, someone who has maintained self-control may finally break out in a flood of tears. I myself have always found it a very moving moment, especially because we are then so close to the edge of that open grave. Nonetheless, I continue to maintain that if we really mean to *bury* our deceased loved one, we should not leave his body, from which the spirit has already departed, lying there on the ground. We should not insist on sparing ourselves the frightfulness of the moment when the casket descends. After all, what is our comfort in relation to that body? With mouth and heart we recite the words of the Apostles Creed: "I believe in the resurrection of the body and the life everlasting." Do we not then pray the very prayer which our Lord taught us, the prayer that contains everything we need now and for eternity?

After the ceremony at the grave, we normally return to the church or the funeral home. There may well be people who now begin to conduct themselves in a different manner than they did during the journey to the open grave. When people walk away from the grave and head back to the church or funeral home, they may talk busily or even laugh out loud. To be honest about it, I find such behavior amazing and even painful. After all, we shouldn't get carried away at such a time.

It seems to me a good practice to end the activities of the burial day in the same manner in which they began, keeping the same Christian style throughout, namely, with a prayer and a short Bible reading. Yet this may not be possible in every case.

He carried the little casket himself

They had been married for about six years, but no children had come. Medical investigation did not turn up any reason why there were no children. Therefore the specialist had told them not to get discouraged. They answered, "We will keep asking the LORD for children." Yes, that's the kind of people they were. They went through a very difficult time of testing in faith. Eventually they experienced what they had long confessed concerning God's wise and providential will, however difficult it became for them.

What a joy it was for them when, some years later, it was medically established that she was expecting a baby. Both the husband and the wife were excited; the congregation rejoiced with them.

He was extremely careful with his wife after that. "You can tell that it's our first baby," she joked. "I'm not made of porcelain."

The pregnancy progressed well. For the entire nine months, the doctor was completely satisfied. Yet as the time for birth drew near, there was tension. The birth came later than the date the doctor had given, although this is not unusual in the case of a first baby.

The birth itself also went well. It happened late at night, but the husband and wife didn't mind. And the doctor arrived in good time. "What a joy! We have received a child from the LORD." That was what the father proclaimed as he held the baby in his arms. "A son to carry on my name."

But then things took a turn for the worse. Within a mere matter of hours, there were some small signs that something was wrong. The baby was not breathing well. Now and then he turned blue.

That same night he died. The doctor was utterly perplexed and telephoned me. Within half an hour, I was with the parents who had so suddenly been plunged into sorrow. Not one of us knew what to say — that's how dejected we felt. There were questions surfacing in our hearts for which we had no answers.

All sorts of feelings rush through you at such a time. O God, *why* is this necessary?

Toward morning we achieved a degree of peace of mind and were able to read Scripture together and pray. The LORD had changed rebellion and incomprehension into a believing desire to unite our will with His as we looked to Him in prayer. With a lump in our throat and tears in our eyes we could confess together that the LORD never makes a mistake.

There were many things to be arranged that morning. The death had to be registered with the authorities. Arrangements for burial had to be made. A carpenter agreed to make a small casket, less than half a meter in length.

It was somewhere between one and two o'clock when the baby's father and I walked over to the cemetery. He carried the little casket on his own broad shoulder. As we stood by the grave, I read a passage of Scripture. The gospel resounded clearly in that cemetery: "The LORD's lovingkindness indeed never ceases, for His compassion never fails . . . if He causes grief, then He will have compassion according to His abundant lovingkindness. For He does not afflict willingly, or grieve the sons of men" (Lam. 3:22, 32–33).

I then proceeded to read from Article 17 of the first chapter of the Canons of Dort: "We must judge concerning the will of God from His Word, which declares that the children of believers are holy, not by nature but in virtue of the covenant of grace, in which they are included with their parents. Therefore, God-fearing parents ought not to doubt the election and salvation of their children whom God calls out of this life in their infancy."

When we got home, I repeated the readings for the benefit of the baby's mother. Then we were able to pray together and give thanks. And together we sang the words of Psalm 89: "I will extol thee, LORD, Thy mercies I will praise, and of Thy steadfast love I'll sing through all my days."

Such sentiments are incomprehensible to a person of darkened intellect. They are only possible through faith. May God be praised!

There were only five of us

He died unexpectedly at an advanced age, when he was almost ninety years old. He had almost no visitors during the final years. His son hardly showed up anymore: he was done with his father. Reconciliation appeared to be out of the question because there had been a quarrel over the matter of taking over the farm: the son had not gotten his way. Another son had died. The widow of the deceased son appeared on the scene only after her father-in-law had died. She wanted to know whether I would be willing to conduct the funeral. There was no reason for me not to do so.

Since it is my practice to read Scripture and lead in prayer after I have talked with family members in such circumstances, I also asked this in her case. She said no. Ever since the death of her husband, she no longer believed. God had made her bitter, and she had turned her back on him.

I explained to her briefly what would happen at the funeral. I would read from the Bible and speak in accordance with the Scriptures. She could hardly object to this, even though I could read on her face that she did not regard it as necessary for herself.

On the afternoon of the funeral, there were only five of us in attendance in a good-sized auditorium: the daughter-in-law with her two sons, the funeral director, and I. The funeral director said to me: "This is hardly worth your effort — make it short." My answer was: "This is going to be a Christian burial of the kind I normally lead, as you know from experience." He remained still, and I proceeded.

The gospel was read and proclaimed. The appeal went out to accept in faith what the LORD demands and promises in His Word. Only when there is such acceptance can there be eternal salvation.

Was it worth the bother of saying these things? Most certainly — especially in this case. The LORD knows very well what He wants and what He is doing.

At such a time you don't think of your faith

Before I visited her, I did not know her. Thus we had to get used to each other at first. Before long she began to open up. Although it had happened some years before, she still had not gotten over it: her husband had been killed very suddenly in a serious automobile accident. He was on his way to the office during rush hour. Another automobile went through a red light and smashed his car. He died instantly.

The police came to bring her the bad news. She didn't even get to see his body because it had been so badly mangled: the people at the hospital strongly advised against it.

In the weeks and months that followed, she lived as if in a dream. At times it was more like a nightmare.

In the lengthy conversation that followed these revelations, I tried to approach her pastorally. At a certain moment I asked: "Didn't your faith give you some support in those difficult times?"

She answered, "Oh, during such a time you don't think about your faith. You have other things on your mind."

Although I understood what she was saying, I found it a strange response. Is it really true that when believers come to such crucial moments in their lives, they do not get support from their faith? I know it can happen that way sometimes, especially if they are overwhelmed with sorrow and do not think things through from the standpoint of faith. It is understandable, all right, but not something of which we should approve.

We talked about this very point for a while. At the end of the conversation I could make clear to her what I meant. She is still very thankful to me for this.

Does God forget to be gracious? Does He lock His mercy away? No, no — a thousand times no! "Thy way, O God, is holy; what god is great like our God?" (Ps. 77:13).

Chapter 11

Abiding Responsibility

> *"And if one member suffers, all the members suffer with it; if one member is honored, all the members rejoice with it. Now you are Christ's body, and individually members of it."*   (I Cor. 12:26–27)

> *"Why are you in despair, O my soul, and why have you become disturbed within me? Hope in God, for I shall yet praise Him, the help of my countenance and my God."*   (Ps. 42:5, 12)

> *"But we do not want you to be uninformed, brethren, about those who are asleep, that you may not grieve, as do the rest who have no hope."*   (I Thess. 4:13)

> *"For we do not have a high priest who cannot sympathize with our weaknesses, but one who has been tempted in all things as we are, yet without sin."*   (Heb. 4:15)

Don't just promise — do it

What I said about people suffering from terminal illnesses applies just as much to their loved ones. Within the communion of the saints, they never appeal in vain to the pastoral concern of the Good Shepherd. Thus they are entitled to continuing care after the crisis has passed. This care must be made available to them by those who minister in their church. There is no place in the church for the infamous attitude demonstrated by Cain when he asked "Am I my brother's keeper?" (Gen. 4:9).

The Church is the Body of Christ. Every person who belongs to the church is a member occupying a unique place within the whole. There are differences in gifts among the various members of the church. What we find is not a colorless uniformity but a colorful pluriformity.

Because of this diversity in gifts, the care extended to those who are working through the grieving process can be intense. Here we see an application of what the apostle Paul says: "And if one member suffers, all the members suffer with it" (I Cor. 12:26).

To suffer along with others is to participate in their lives. I wrote on this theme earlier: further commentary should not be needed here.

It is our custom to assure the loved ones of a person who has died that we share their loss. For the family such an assurance can be helpful, but it also represents a test — especially if the pain caused by the unexpected tragic loss is very great and the line of persons presenting condolences is very long. We have to use some common sense in these matters.

In these situations what happens is that we not only encourage the bereaved but also make promises to them. "I'll come and look you up" or "I won't leave you all alone" or "If you need any help, all you have to do is give me a call."

It's a wonderful thing that you make such promises — provided they are not mere expressions of feelings that you meant sincerely when you voiced them but then forgot half an hour later. Sometimes we get carried away by the pain being suffered by the bereaved family. We need to remember that if we promise something, we must also do it.

In this context a question arises. Has it struck you that a minister sometimes says at the end of a funeral service, "Be sure you don't forget those who have been left alone?" Such an urgent appeal for "abiding responsibility" seems to be needed quite often, I'm sorry to say.

This responsibility is often felt and discharged by people in the weeks immediately following the burial. But what happens after that? What happens when almost no one comes to visit the bereaved any more?

Of course I'm aware that the course of normal life is soon resumed. And nowadays everyone is very busy with various tasks and assignments in the church or civic life or society. That's why we should reflect on some familiar words: "This is pure and undefiled religion in the sight of our God and Father, to visit orphans and widows in their distress, and to keep oneself unstained by the world" (James 1:27).

That's literally what we read in God's Word. And the Word is the norm for our life, also in such a matter as this. Does it apply to the way church members relate to each other? Let's remember the promises we have made!

The nature and course of the grieving process

There is hardly anyone who gets over a loss right away. The believer is not an exception to this rule. If he loses one of his most precious possessions, such as his house or his automobile, he has some feelings to work through. He has to find a way to deal with them, and it will take some time.

This is all the more true when the loss is that of the person who was closest to us. We had been bound to that person for many years with the most intimate bonds, whether as "one flesh" (marriage) or as our own blood (parents or children).

The process of working through such a loss is called grieving. The nature of this process is determined by the fact that separation is painful. Even if the pain is not intense, the process takes time.

The process is a lot like the series of phases which a dying person goes through. Yet as we consider such stages or phases, we should never forget that people are not all alike. The separate stages must not be regarded as a fixed scheme. And it is worth emphasizing that one should not approach such situations from a theoretical point of view. In other words, a person offering pastoral assistance would do well to bear in mind that not all human beings go through the grieving process in exactly the same way.

A loss that affects us deeply places us in a unique situation. The process begins with a shock effect, especially if the loss was unexpected and disturbing. We lose our equilibrium somewhat; we need time to become ourselves again. But some never quite return to what they were. Even if they take refuge in the Lord every day and draw on their faith as a resource, there remains a wound that causes constant pain.

Someone who suffers a very serious loss runs the risk of being buried under his sorrow. He may go through a serious trauma. The loss of a marriage partner can have grave consequences. I have seen it happen more than once that someone who lost a marriage partner went through life — especially at first — acting numbed and stupefied. The actions that make up daily life were carried out in automatic fashion; the person performing them did not seem to be involved.

Along with loneliness there can be an unwillingness to speak. This makes sense when you think about it. When you are left alone after many years of happy marriage, you miss the daily pleasant conversations and the partner who takes an interest in you: there are no more discussions of what went on in church, or of the meeting of this or that society, or of a story on the front page of the newspaper.

Just think for a moment what it means to be without someone who answers you when you speak. It is as though the sun has vanished from the house. You just sit there staring. You have no purpose anymore, no desire to get up and be active. The walls seem to close you in. You have lost your support, your helper. After this you must do everything on your own. And if you're not used to it and don't know how to do some of the things that need doing, then what?

Don't look back — look ahead

"It's easy for you to talk. You still have your husband (or your wife). But what about me? I have *lost* the person who was dearest to me. Unless you have experienced such a loss directly, you're in no position to talk with me about it."

Every now and then someone speaks to me this way. Such a person is at the very deepest point in the grieving process.

In a certain sense, of course, the person who talks this way is right. We simply must admit that it's very difficult for us to place ourselves in the feelings of someone else. To acknowledge this at once and to show that you mean it does a good deal to further pastoral contact.

On the other hand, we must not allow such remarks to deter us from our pastoral task. We must be especially careful not to not fall in with the train of thought and style of expression that belongs to the person we are trying to help. A wise and careful approach will only prove possible if we do our best to offer help *along Biblical lines*. We must speak in the awareness that we have God's Word in hand — and then point to that Word.

What we say must be in accordance with that Word. If we fail in this regard, we might as well stay home for all the good we will do.

What is really your intention? Surely you want to offer real help to the brother or sister who is in need. You want to help him or her get over the roughest spot in the grieving process.

Now, the psalms are full of helpful passages. We see that the believers of the Old Covenant era repeatedly called out to the LORD in their need; they asked Him for deliverance, for insight, for perspective. How gloriously the God of the covenant heard and answered! O God, Thou hast placed me in wide open spaces and hast revived me and enabled me to breathe again.

Think of the writer of Psalm 42. How genuinely he expresses the ultimate deliverance of the soul that yearns for God, the *living* God. Twice he emphatically tells us what gives rest to the soul that is bent low and disturbed — hope in God. "Why are you in despair, O my soul? And why have you become disturbed within me? Hope in God" (vs. 5). Yes, He picks up those who are cast down, gives courage to those who are weary, and revives the spirits of those who feel defeated. The psalm concludes: "I shall yet praise Him, the help of my countenance and my God" (vs. 12).

By looking to God in faith, we also gain perspective. The sense of loss does not go away and the wound still causes us pain, but we do not look exclusively at what lies *behind* us, at what we have lost; no, we begin to look *ahead*. We begin to understand that the LORD still wants to use us as His workbench, and that we should be no less active than before. Slowly but surely we discover that we are interested in the events of our own life and the things around us. We find ourselves reading church papers and newspapers again. We receive visitors and begin to attend society meetings. There are times when we are amazed at ourselves. We have found our equilibrium again!

People are miserable comforters

Why is this? We would rather visit people who are getting married than people who are mourning. We would rather offer congratulations than condolences. We dread the prospect of visiting a family where there has been a death.

There are various reasons that could be mentioned. We shudder at the very thought of death. The pain and sorrow of others also causes us to lose our equilibrium somewhat. We do not quite know how to conduct ourselves in relation to people who have suffered such deadly disappointments; we do not know what to say to them. We feel powerless and speechless.

Such reactions are common. People trained to offer pastoral assistance have the same feelings. In a certain sense, however, there is something commendable about such feelings: they are an indication of how much we, as members of the same body as the bereaved, wish to share their feelings and sufferings with them. We admit that we are weakened and discouraged just as they are. We are ready to stand *alongside* them.

When we bear these considerations in mind, we see that an attitude of dread toward visiting the bereaved should not surprise us; rather, it is a reason for joy. It shows that we are not above the sorrows of others. Those sorrows also affect *us* and cause *us* pain.

People are miserable comforters. Therefore it is wise not to force things or run the risk of being artificial. The need for such restraint applies both to ourselves as would-be comforters and to the bereaved whom we visit in order to offer encouragement. A pastor has to learn this too. Offering support to people in mourning is often not easy for him, even if he has to do this a hundred times or more in his career as a pastor. If he knows himself and knows the needs of the bereaved, he also realizes that he, of himself, is a miserable comforter. If he is a good pastor, he will never get accustomed to this part of his service in office. For him it will never become a matter of routine! We should be thankful for this.

What do you do, then, as minister? At first you might do nothing more than listen. Let the grieving family give expression to its anxieties. And whatever you do, don't hit them with those facile assurances that bring the conversation to a sudden end. Stay on the same level as the sheep entrusted to your care by the Good Shepherd, and make sure you are aware of their feelings and spiritual capacities. Don't try to give them something they won't be able to work through. And bear in mind that when they are grieving, there may be a number of matters that need their attention.

The bereaved feel strengthened when we let them know that they don't stand alone in their grief. We show them that the LORD shares their sorrows and ministers to them by means of His servants. This realization opens up space for a good conversation.

Not all situations are alike

I mentioned earlier that in some situations one can proceed quite quickly to have a good conversation with the family members of someone who has died — perhaps right after the death has taken place. One should then build on that conversation when offering subsequent pastoral care, remembering to point out that in Jesus Christ "we do not have a high priest who cannot sympathize with our weaknesses, but one who has been tempted in all things as we are, yet without sin" (Heb. 4:15).

I have observed a number of times, also to my own comfort, how families in mourning are gripped by the very familiar words of the apostle Paul: "We do not want you to be uninformed, brethren, about those who are asleep, that you may not grieve, as do the rest who have no hope" (I Thess. 4:13).

There is also sorrow that has not been worked through, a sorrow in which the mourners must first discover themselves. We often encounter such sorrow among older people who have a hard time expressing themselves, perhaps those in whom there remains something of what was learned in their youth. They try to act brave and do not let others see their sorrow — they think it is expected of them. They work hard to maintain self-control. They bottle it up. They do not complain but suffer in silence and pray for strength.

In some ways I can respect what these people do. On the other hand, I confront them, for I know they are having a very hard time. It's just that they don't want anyone to see or sense what they are going through. In the church it ought to be regarded as a commendable deed to pour out your heart to someone whom you can trust, someone who clearly stands ready to help you.

It is important to point out that accepting your situation and loss is different than acquiescing in it. The latter is a passive response, as if one were saying, "I cannot change what God has done, and so I bend under His chastising hand." This might sound like a humble attitude, but actually it is not. The LORD hates such an attitude. He teaches us that He does indeed cause wounds but also stands ready to pour oil over those wounds and heal them!

Not all losses are equally difficult

The sober attitude that is called for in our pastoral work must also reckon with this reality. It is simply a fact. As we see people working through their grief in the mourning process, we observe that there are degrees and gradations of mourning. The intensity of the sorrow is partly conditioned by the magnitude of the loss: the tighter the bonds with the one who has died, the deeper the feeling of pain will be. For example, the death of a young child who loved life will cause different emotions than the death of a very aged grandmother who was suffering greatly or was mentally handicapped.

Men go through the grieving process in a different way than women. They usually express themselves differently as well. This does not mean that they take things lightly or that they are not deeply affected by a death; it's just that a man's way of reacting is not the same as a woman's. Women sometimes have an easier time working through the grieving process than men.

It is obvious that every case is somewhat unique and has to be judged and interpreted in terms of the specific circumstances of the person doing the grieving. This is part of the reason why people offering pastoral assistance need a knowledge of human nature and should possess considerable wisdom about life in general. All too often we fall short in this regard.

As pastors we must also be aware that with God we have such a high priest as the one I discussed a little earlier. The person offering pastoral assistance is just as much in need of help as the people he is helping.

The big blow was yet to come

The young wife had only been married for a few years when her husband died suddenly. The one minute they were sitting together and having a cozy chat, and the next minute he was gone.

People said it must have been "cardiac arrest." Although this term does not explain everything, it did seem to be justified in such a case. Generally speaking, people cannot survive after their heart has stopped beating. People have to have something to say at such a time — therefore we should not quarrel with them over such a term as "cardiac arrest."

What was more obvious was that the young widow was being very brave. After the initial shock she quickly recovered her composure. There was so much to be done — call the doctor, notify the relatives, bring the children over to the neighbors, and so forth.

Yes, she certainly was brave! Visitors could talk with her calmly about her husband's sudden death. From the things she said, it was apparent that her marriage had been a very happy one. For this she had reason to be thankful to the LORD, who now showed that He remained faithful to her.

She manifested the same calm during the funeral and at the graveside. You simply had to see her standing there with her two small children. It was a moving sight. There were no tears. Most of us were happy to note this, for we had prayed that God would give her strength.

A few shook their heads compassionately. They thought to themselves: this is not normal — the big blow is yet to come. You know the kind of person I'm talking about: the one who always knows better. You find such people everywhere.

But these "know-it-alls" were not proven right. Too bad for them! Perhaps they will learn something — that not every grieving process follows the path they have so nicely laid out.

For months the young mother with her children was supported on all sides. The relatives, the neighbors, the members of the church — they all showed themselves willing to help. It was something tremendous. All this care was helping her to deal with her painful loss.

And yet, brave as she was at the outset, she found after some months that she was tired and depressed — especially when she was alone. Often she would weep during the night.

She told me about it during one of my visits to her. She really didn't want anyone to know about it, because she was afraid to create the impression that she was not trusting fully in the LORD. There was no need for worry in this regard, for she was indeed trusting in Him.

By telling her a few things which I drew from my own experience as a pastor, I was able to set her mind at ease. At the same time I urged her not to feel obliged to put up a false front. She should allow others to see her as she really was. After all, we human beings are all fundamentally the same. If we are weak in ourselves, we can still be strong in the Lord.

Those who had shaken their heads knowingly did not get to say, "I told you so." Even so, I am convinced that if they knew what I had come to know, they would not have understood it. They were too short-sighted to see what really goes on in such a case. They would have looked at each other knowingly and said, "See, didn't we say all along that for her the big blow was yet to come?" Just let them talk — those people who think they know it all!

My mommy is in heaven

Our brother was left behind with four young children. The oldest was eight, and the youngest was not yet two. His unmarried sister had been looking after the housekeeping for some months already. That aspect was going well.

Although he had been prepared for the death of his wife, he took it hard. For the first so many days, he lived as if in a dream. Of course he could not just throw in the towel: there were the children who needed his full attention.

After a week's leave, he had to go back to his regular job at the office. His friends did not expect him to fend for himself altogether, but they didn't run in and out all the time either. They gave him opportunity to rest, so that he could recover and regain his equilibrium. He was to do so in God's strength, of course, but it isn't always necessary to add these words.

It was very difficult for him to play with the children. His wife had always enjoyed games with the children, and so the prospect of playing with them intensified his sense of loss!

And the children — especially the younger ones — asked questions: "Where *is* our mommy now? With the Lord Jesus? But where is He then? In heaven? Is that far away? Way up there in the sky? Somewhere behind the clouds? Is it nice there? We'll be there one day too, won't we, Daddy? Then we will all be together again."

I found him at home on a day off. The younger children were home with him. They knew me well and even addressed me as "Uncle." They sat on my knee while I talked with their father, who was making coffee.

Suddenly the five-year-old boy ran outside. He said I was to come with him to the back yard. "Look, Uncle, do you see the clouds?

Mommy is behind them now. She's in heaven with the Lord Jesus. And Daddy says we will also be allowed to go there some day. Isn't that great?"

I had to swallow before I could speak. This little boy's faith put many older ones to shame. I was reminded of what the Savior said: "Truly I say to you, whoever does not receive the kingdom of God like a child shall not enter it at all" (Luke 18:17). At that moment I knew what I would preach on when Sunday came around!

He was plagued with painful guilt feelings

It was a family like many others today. The father worked for a large, well-known company. He was an excellent salesman and was away from home a great deal, sometimes for a number of days in succession. His work, which he enjoyed greatly, took him out of the country on occasion. His evenings were largely taken up with other tasks. He was a deacon and took his office seriously. He regularly visited the families in his district. People who appealed to him for help were never turned away. He was the president of this and the secretary of that. You know how it is: if you are enthusiastic and zealous, you soon find yourself involved in all sorts of things.

It did bother him that his wife rarely got to see him or talk with him, but he did not realize what this really meant for her. The raising of the children was largely left to her. And it was by no means a light responsibility — especially when the children began to reach the difficult years. Somehow parents have to pull them through the hard times and keep them from being hurt — after all, isn't that what they promised at baptism?

The mother carried her responsibilities without complaining. As much as possible, she surrendered her husband to his other involvements. To friends and the minister and her district elder, she justified his being away from home so much. "He enjoys the work," she explained, "and he's certainly cut out for it. Of course, he's working for the church and the kingdom of God." She was a wonderful woman — and our brother knew it.

But some of us had our own ideas about the situation. I once asked the man straight out, "Aren't you neglecting your task as head of your family?" I could see from the way he looked at me that he knew he was in the wrong, and he immediately promised that he would do better.

But the next day he was back in the same pattern: he enjoyed his work and did things his own way. He basked in the appreciation he met with at work and also received for his involvement in Christian society life. Was he the kind of person who needs to be stroked regularly? It seemed to me that if he wanted appreciation, he should have stayed home with his wife and gotten more of it there.

He was enjoying himself, then. But it was not to last much longer. Once again he was outside the country, just a little ways over the border. When he came back to his hotel after a business appointment, a telegram was handed to him: "Come straight home. Wife gravely ill." She died that same day.

It is hard to describe the mourning process this brother went through. He seemed to fall into an abyss in which he was plagued with painful guilt feelings. He continually thought to himself: "If only I had been home more often these last years! If only I had paid more attention to my wife and children! If only I had listened to the minister! If only I had cut down on all that traveling and organizational work and concentrated on my primary calling! I was supposed to be a father and a husband."

And now? It was too late. God, he thought, had punished him severely. He could never make up for it. His conscience would not allow him a moment's rest. Many times he was close to utter despair. Self-reproach and remorse can be very hard to endure — especially when there is good reason to feel guilty.

I talked with him a great deal. It took a long time before he could believe that divine forgiveness was available for him too — for Christ's sake. His joy at the realization that he was forgiven remained tempered, for he could not set aside the thought that in this life he would have no opportunity to confess his shortcomings to his wife. He never seemed to achieve peace on that score, for when I encountered him again years later, he immediately brought it up.

Chapter 12

Above — Not Underneath

> *"These things I have spoken to you, that in me you may have peace. In the world you have tribulation, but take courage; I have overcome the world."*
>
> (John 16:33)

> *"How blessed are the people who know the joyful sound! O LORD, they walk in the light of Thy countenance. In Thy name they rejoice all the day, and by Thy righteousness they are exalted."* (Ps. 89:15–16)

> *"Hallelujah! For the Lord our God, the Almighty, reigns. Let us rejoice and be glad and give the glory to Him, for the marriage of the Lamb has come and His bride has made herself ready."* (Rev. 19:6–7)

> *"And the Spirit and the Bride say, 'Come.' And let the one who hears say, 'Come.' And let the one who is thirsty come; let the one who wishes take the water of life without cost."* (Rev. 22:17)

The brokenness of life

Not one can deny this reality. We are confronted with it daily in our own environment and our own life. And we see that the brokenness extends far beyond the boundaries of our own country. In this regard, the images on television speak to us clearly. There is so much suffering and misery all over the world that we sometimes ask in despair: How can God permit these things? Why doesn't He intervene?

Some people say that every house has its own cross. To stick with our subject, pastoral workers (in the limited sense explained earlier, i.e.

those to whom the care of terminal patients is entrusted) know from their experience how heavy that cross can be for people on their deathbed as they experience pain and anguish of both body and soul. They are subjected to temptations, and they begin to doubt. Or they cannot bear the consequences of their ailment. But there can also be despair among the immediate family members, who cannot bear to see their loved one suffering. Do not underestimate the weight of the cross which those loved ones must bear!

When we see all this brokenness, what is the most difficult thing of all for us? It is to experience what we confess.

From the very earliest days we know that such experience is needed. We also know how it comes — not through seemingly superhuman spiritual powers of our own, but only in Christ's power. We need not bear our cross alone. We may cast all our cares on the One who suffered on the cross for all of us.

Does this help? Our pain, sorrow and suffering are not thereby made less. There are even people who, in such a situation, begin to doubt the genuineness of their faith, and then they get into still deeper difficulties. Others become bitter because believing and praying do not seem to help.

Can we really experience what we confess when we are confronted with the brokenness of life in our own immediate situation? Is it possible at all? If so, how?

Perfect only in Christ

We can certainly form a vivid mental picture of a reaction like the one discussed above. I can testify that this sort of thing is by no means foreign to my experience.

What we must understand and accept is that God's Word with its rich promises is not to be understood as a set of objective givens which can be embraced as reliable and applicable to our lives only through our own subjective experience. If that's how matters stood, it would depend upon *us* as to what we experience and ultimately believe.

Scripture does not provide any basis for any such "experiential theology," of which we see so much among Christians today. God's Word *is* the Truth, even if not one person acknowledges it. And that Word, laden with the power of His Spirit, will itself ensure that it is made true in our lives. We read in the Canons of Dort: ". . . regeneration is not inferior in power to creation or the resurrection of the dead" (Ch. III–IV, Art. 12). Our creed then goes on to affirm: "Therefore the will so renewed is not only acted upon and moved by God but, acted upon by God, the will itself also acts. Hence also man himself is rightly said to believe and repent through the grace he has received." Thanks to that grace, we can be of good courage in all circumstances.

But someone might object and say that God's children are also able to lose hope. They can be bent low under the burdens they must bear in this "vale of tears." They can be "broken," deeply disappointed within, rebellious, or despairing. If so, what about those works of God which never fail? Is it really the case that the One who has promised is always faithful in carrying out His promises?

In response we must affirm that God indeed fulfils His promises. This is something we should not doubt for a moment. But as long as we are in this life, our (human) reactions will be imperfect. We have only a small beginning of the obedience God asks of us.

This realization must not, however, make us passive. Neither is it a valid excuse when, as happens so often, we fall into sin or come up short in terms of obedience. On the contrary, when it comes to the "small beginning," we should remember what we confess concerning those who have been regenerated: ". . . with earnest purpose they do begin to live not only according to some but to all the commandments of God" (Heidelberg Catechism, Answer 114).

In this way we can indeed experience what we confess. The apostle Paul says it so clearly with regard to himself and to us: "Not that I have already obtained it, or have already become perfect, but I press on in order that I may lay hold of that for which also I was laid hold of by Christ Jesus" (Phil 3:12). Note his appeal: "Let us therefore, as many as are perfect, have this attitude . . ." (vs. 15).

Are you *already* perfect? Yes, but only *in* Christ, in communion with Him. In this way we can indeed rest in the Lord when it comes to the greatest sorrows in our hearts. In Christ we then have peace with God and with our "lot" in life. And when the consequences of our fall into sin become painful experiences for us in daily life (I think here of suffering, oppression, sorrow, and pain), we are of good cheer, for Christ has assured us: "In the world you have tribulation, but take courage; I have overcome the world" (John 16:33).

Rejoicing all the day

What I just wrote takes some time to understand and absorb. But there is still more to be said. Even before we are baptized, a moving prayer is raised on our behalf in the congregation, as part of the baptism form.

This form includes a section that raises questions in the minds of some people. The following prayer to the LORD occurs: "We pray that he (she), following Him day by day, may joyfully bear his (her) cross and cleave to Him in true faith, firm hope, and ardent love."

Thus it appears that we are to bear our cross *joyfully!* But isn't it true that in many difficult situations we fall far short of this ideal? What are we to make of this matter?

There are indeed many places in Scripture where an appeal is made to be happy or joyful. The joy that is spoken of in such passages does not exist on its own; rather, it results from fellowship with God in His covenant — it is joy in the Lord! The apostle Paul writes: "Rejoice in the Lord always; again I will say, rejoice!" (Phil. 4:4).

The apostle James writes: "Consider it all joy, my brethren, when you encounter various trials" (James 1:2). James lets us know that we are tempted on a daily basis by the "big three," our arch-enemies, namely, the devil, the world, and our own flesh. We are always in the midst of the battle. But are we really supposed to regard this challenge as a reason for joy? Read further and note what the apostle is talking about: "knowing that the testing of your faith produces endurance" (vs. 3).

David spoke to the LORD about those who were rebellious toward Him and asked Him to bring them to destruction through their own devices. He went on to say: "But let all who take refuge in Thee be glad, let them ever sing for joy; and mayest Thou shelter them, that those who love Thy name may exult in Thee. For it is Thou who dost bless the righteous man, O LORD, Thou dost surround him with favor as with a shield" (Ps. 5:11–12).

Are we to rejoice in the battle? Yes indeed, for the LORD is at our right hand. It should be our daily joy to be allowed to love and serve the Lord. It should be pure joy for us to experience that *He* is the one "who pardons all your iniquities; who heals all your diseases; who redeems your life from the pit; who crowns you with lovingkindness and compassion; who satisfies your years with good things, so that your youth is renewed like the eagle" (Ps. 103:3–5). Therefore we say with the psalmist: "Bless the LORD, O my soul, and forget none of His benefits" (vs. 2).

True joy makes it possible for us to bear our cross or our suffering cheerfully. True joy sanctifies our pain. Therefore the psalmist proclaims: "How blessed are the people who know the joyful sound! O LORD, they walk in the light of Thy countenance. In Thy name they rejoice all the day, and by Thy righteousness they are exalted" (Ps. 89:15–16).

Rejoicing all the day, being cheerful at all times — yes, in the God of our salvation. We rejoice in Him, who for our sakes humbled Himself and was obedient to the point of death on the cross (Phil. 2:8).

We suffer a great deal of pain. We sit with tears in our eyes at a deathbed, and we are deeply moved when we stand by an open grave. But, thanks be to God, we do not go underneath it. Rather, in our spiritual battle we find that we are not defeated by it but that we have *already overcome it* — we are already above it, thanks to Christ.

The congregation prayed for us when we were baptized and asked that it would be possible for us to bear our cross joyfully. But how is such a thing possible? By clinging in true faith, firm hope and ardent love to Him, whom we desire and love. Has the LORD ever forsaken anyone who clung to Him in prayer?

Ready for the wedding feast

Happy the people who know the joyful sound! God's children are to be congratulated once they have learned that they must at all times rejoice in the Lord. When they do so, they taste the beginning of eternal happiness.

It is good to point this out. The proclamation of the praise of the LORD has not been emphasized as it should have been. The entire creation in all of its parts cries out in labor pains to be delivered. With deep longing it waits for the revelation of the sons of God. Thus the sighing of the creation has a purpose. The creation knows that the hour of liberation from its barrenness is coming. It knows that the time is approaching when the total deliverance of God's people will be a fact.

Thus not only the creation but "we ourselves, having the first fruits of the Spirit, even we ourselves groan within ourselves, waiting eagerly for our adoption as sons, the redemption of our body" (Rom. 8:23). That's how strongly we should desire the moment when all things are made new.

It is not hard to see that this longing must be combined with an everyday readiness for the wedding feast. What I mean by this is not some out-of-the-ordinary posture of readiness but an ordinary living out of faith for the honor of God.

After all, shouldn't we be proclaiming God's great deeds under all circumstances? Shouldn't we talk about how we are led by our High Priest and Teacher, who is the Head of His Church? That's no small thing — to be chosen and to be formed as part of the age-old and world-wide choir that is the Church, which sings united praises to God's mighty deeds of redemption and re-creation.

Whoever truly believes does not, then, remain standing on his own. Because he glories in God and sings the praises of His infallible Word, he unites himself with the choir that is Christ's bride.

Any and all who ignore this truth are acting against God's command (see Article 28 of the Belgic Confession). If this being able to sing together applies to *the present*, we must actively practice the communion of the saints. Those who are well may not for a moment act as though they can get along without the members of the body who are ill — or vice versa.

The living and the dying, in their dependence on the one Lord, know that they belong together. In the way they live as well as in the way they die, believers show that they are ready for the wedding feast. Those who offer pastoral assistance will thus have to share in the distribution of the treasures and gifts which we possess for Christ's sake. We do not distribute those gifts in a greedy way, or in an abstemious or reluctant way, but with generosity and a heart full of joy — showing ourselves to be truly concerned and caring.

Under the faultless and powerful leading of Christ, we must then turn our hearts to one another and see to it that we come across as a *harmonious* group and choir. It is in this way that we work toward the marriage feast of the Lamb and the eternal hallelujah.

Then we will give substance to something that the apostle John was once privileged to see and hear for our sakes: "Hallelujah! For the Lord our God, the Almighty, reigns. Let us rejoice and be glad and give the glory to Him, for the marriage of the Lamb has come and His bride has made herself ready" (Rev. 19:6–7).

The fervent longing of the Spirit and the Bride

In Revelation 22 we are assured expressly by the glorified Christ that He will soon return. He is already underway, for He is the Coming One.

Naturally, the Church looks forward with deep desire to His coming. After all, she is Christ's bride!

That desire becomes manifest in our daily prayers. The Holy Spirit helps us in this regard, for He prays for us with "groanings too deep for words" (Rom. 8:26).

Now, the fiery desire of the Spirit and the Bride are not confined to moments of pious reflection. Neither is our life of prayer to be separated from our deeds. Everything we do and refrain from doing should be regarded as pervaded by our prayer for the Lord's return.

The apostle Peter made this clear to us. After pointing out that all things are to pass away to make way for a new heaven and a new earth, he asks: ". . . what sort of people ought you to be in holy conduct and godliness, looking for and hastening the coming of the day of God?" (I Pet. 3:11–12).

Our fervent desire for Christ's return, together with the Spirit, does not remain confined to our "prayer chamber." Neither is it a personalistic experience cut off from the Church's "Maranatha" cry. Remember what Peter told us: "Therefore, beloved, since you look for these things, be diligent to be found by Him in peace, spotless and blameless" (vs. 14).

*   *   *   *   *

"And the Spirit and the bride say, 'Come.' And let the one who hears say, 'Come.' And let the one who is thirsty come; let the one who wishes take the water of life without cost" (Rev. 22:17).

Note that the Spirit is mentioned first here. He shows us the way, sets the tone, gives us the insight we need, and provides us with the will and capacity to testify — in everything we do — to our yearning for the Lord's return.

This desire must come to expression in *deeds*: it must not remain without fruit. The insistent plea "Come, Lord Jesus" will be taken over by those who notice that the desire leads to action. It will become an ever more ecumenical prayer, one which governs our practice of the communion of saints and stimulates us to show mercy to the seriously ill and to those who are dying of terminal diseases.

The healthy and the sick, the living and the dying — they are all dependent on reconciliation with God through Jesus Christ. They can all be saved and live forever if in faith they draw from the Source of the water of life — Christ.

When we care for the dying along Scriptural lines and accompany them during their final days, we are giving them the very best care that people with terminal diseases can possibly get. Let those who need this kind of care at the end of their life on earth drink from the ultimate

Source of life. Let them enjoy the water which Christ pours out for them *without cost.*

What an encouraging and strengthening power there is in this water! Those needing help and those giving the help can then hold each other by the hand in the firm conviction of faith: "Thou hast taken hold of my right hand. With Thy counsel Thou wilt guide me, and afterward receive me to glory" (Ps. 73:23–24). Then we can hold our heads high, for through Him, and Him alone, for the sake of His good pleasure, we are destined to wear the crown of glory.

＊   ＊   ＊   ＊   ＊

> O Holy Spirit, precious gift
> Thou Comforter unfailing,
> From Satan's snares our souls uplift,
> And let Thy power, availing,
> Avert our woes and calm our dread.
> For us the Saviour's blood was shed;
> We trust in Thee to keep us.

Through the words of this familiar hymn we are reminded that when the great challenge comes, we are to rise above it, and not go underneath it!

Conclusion

I am thankful that I had the opportunity and encouragement to write these chapters in "my own way." I hope that I have not come across to readers as proud or boastful.

The facts and situations which I passed on by way of illustration are drawn from actual practice. But I have told the stories here in such a manner that no confidentiality of the minister's office was breached.

This little book is meant to be helpful in the sense of offering pastoral perspectives. It is intended for both office-bearers and the members of the congregation, for the latter will, from time to time, receive the office-bearers as they discharge their pastoral responsibilities. I hope and pray that the book will be found helpful by those who offer pastoral help and by people who are dying of terminal illnesses — especially the latter. When the visiting pastor and the dying person can come to agreement on the kinds of things discussed in this book, they are both helped and strengthened!

Other Books from Inheritance Publications

Israel's Hope and Expectation by **Rudolf Van Reest**

G. Nederveen in *Clarion*: This is one of the best novels I have read of late. I found it captivating and hard to put down. Here is a book that is not time-bound and therefore it will never be outdated.

The story takes place around the time of Jesus' birth. It is written by someone who has done his research about the times between the Old and New Testament period. The author informs you in an easy style about the period of the Maccabees.

. . . Van Reest is a good storyteller. His love for the Bible and biblical times is evident from the start. He shows a good knowledge of the customs and mannerisms in Israel. Many fine details add to the quality of the book. You will be enriched in your understanding of the ways in the Old Testament.

for age 14 - 99   **ISBN 0-921100-22-1 Can.$19.95 U.S.$17.90**

Against the World - The Odyssey of Athanasius by **Henry W. Coray**

Muriel R. Lippencott in *The Christian Observer*:

[it] . . . is a partially fictionalized profile of the life of Athanasius . . . who died in 373 AD. Much of the historical content is from the writing of reliable historians. Some parts of the book, while the product of the author's imagination, set forth accurately the spirit and the temper of the times, including the proceedings and vigorous debates that took place in Alexandria and Nicea. . . This is the story that Rev. Coray so brilliantly tells.

for age 14 - 99   **ISBN 0-921100-35-3 Can.$8.95 U.S.$7.90**

Augustine, The Farmer's Boy of Tagaste by **P. De Zeeuw, J.Gzn**

C. MacDonald in *The Banner of Truth*: Augustine was one of the great teachers of the Christian Church, defending it against many heretics. This interesting publication should stimulate and motivate all readers to extend their knowledge of Augustine and his works.

J. Sawyer in *Trowel & Sword*: . . . It is informative, accurate historically and theologically, and very readable. My daughter loved it (and I enjoyed it myself). An excellent choice for home and church libraries.

for age 9 - 99   **ISBN 0-921100-05-1 Can.$7.95 U.S.$6.90**

This Was John Calvin by **Thea B. Van Halsema**

J.H. Kromminga: "Though it reads as smoothly as a well written novel, it is crammed with important facts. It is scholarly and popular at the same time. The book will hold the interest of the young but will also bring new information to the well informed . . . . This book recognizes the true greatness of the man without falling into distortions of the truth to protect that greatness."

It has been translated into Spanish, Portuguese, and Indonesian. This is its fourth printing.

for age 12 - 99   **IP1179 Can.$9.95 U.S.$7.95**

William of Orange - The Silent Prince by **W.G. Van de Hulst**

F. Pronk in *The Messenger*: If you have ever wondered why Dutch Reformed people of former generations felt such strong spiritual ties with Dutch royalty, this is a "must" reading. In simple story form, understandable for children ages 10 and up, the Dutch author, wellknown for Christian children's literature, relates the true story of the origin of Dutch royalty. It all began with William of Nassau (1533-1584) . . . He dedicated his life and lost it for the cause of maintaining and promoting Protestantism in the Netherlands.

for age 9 - 99   **ISBN 0-921100-15-9 Can.$8.95 U.S.$7.90**

Love in Times of Reformation by **William P. Balkenende**

G. Van Dalen in *The Trumpet*: This historical novel plays in the Netherlands during the rise of the protestant Churches, under the persecution of Spain, in the latter half of the sixteenth century. Breaking with the Roman Catholic Church in favor of the new faith is for many an intense struggle. Anthony Tharret, the baker's apprentice, faces his choice before the R.C. Church's influenced Baker's Guild. His love for Jeanne la Solitude, the French Huguenot refugee, gives a fresh dimension to the story. Recommended! Especially for young people.

for age 14 - 99   **ISBN 0-921100-32-9 Can.$8.95 U.S.$7.90**

When The Morning Came by Piet Prins
Struggle for Freedom Series 1

D. Engelsma in the *Standard Bearer*: This is reading for Reformed children, young people, and (if I am any indication) their parents. It is the story of 12-year old Martin Meulenberg and his family during the Roman Catholic persecution of the Reformed Christians in the Netherlands about the year 1600. A peddlar, secretly distributing Reformed books from village to village, drops a copy of Guido de Brès' *True Christian Confession* — a booklet forbidden by the Roman Catholic authorities. An evil neighbor sees the book and informs . . .

for age 9 - 99   **ISBN 0-921100-12-4 Can.\$9.95 U.S.\$8.90**

Three Men Came To Heidelberg
and *Glorious Heretic* by Thea B. Van Halsema

From the sixteenth-century Protestant Reformation came two outstanding statements of Faith: The Heidelberg Catechism (1563) and the Belgic Confession (1561). The stories behind these two historic documents are in this small book.

Frederick, a German prince, asked a preacher and a professor to meet at Heidelberg to write a statement of faith . . . The writer of the Belgic Confession was a hunted man most of his life. Originally he wrote the confession as an appeal to the King of Spain . . .

for age 12 - 99   **IP1610 Can.\$7.95 U.S.\$5.95**

William III and the Revolution of 1688
and *Gustavus Adolphus II*
2 Historical Essays by Marjorie Bowen.

F.G. Oosterhoff in *Reformed Perspective*:

I recommend this book without any hesitation. The two biographies make excellent reading, and the times the essays describe are of considerable interest and importance in the history of our civilization. Moreover, although Bowen obviously is not one in faith with Gustavus Adolphus and William of Orange, her essays relate incidents that are testimonials to God's mercies in preserving His Church. Remembering these mercies, we may take courage for the present and for the future.

for age 13 - 99   **ISBN 0-921100-06-X Can.\$9.95 U.S.\$7.95**

I Will Maintain by Marjorie Bowen
William & Mary Trilogy, Volume 1

The life of William III, Prince of Orange, Stadtholder of the United Netherlands, and King of England is one of the most fascinating in all of History. Both author and publisher of this book had many years of interest in the subject. Even though the story as told in this book is partly fictional, all the main events are faithful to history.

"I challenge all our histories to produce a Prince in all respects his equal; I call the differing humours, interest, and religions of the world to witness whether they ever found a man to centre in, like him . . .

"He might have raised his seat upon his native country's liberty, his very enemies would have supported him in those pretences; but he affected no honours but what were freely offered him, there or elsewhere. . .

"And his ambition, that was only useful, knew how to wear, as well as how to deserve them."

          — WILLIAM FLEETWOOD, Bishop of St. Asaph, *Sermon*

"Since Octavius the world had seen no such instance of precocious statesmanship."

          — LORD MACAULAY, *History of England.*
          ISBN 0-921100-42-6 Can.\$17.95 U.S.\$15.90

The Escape - The Adventures of Three Huguenot Children
Fleeing Persecution by A. Van der Jagt

F. Pronk in *The Messenger*: This book . . . will hold its readers spell-bound from beginning to end. The setting is late seventeenth century France. Early in the story the mother dies and the father is banished to be a galley slave for life on a war ship. Yet in spite of threats and punishment, sixteen-year-old John and his ten-year-old sister Manette, refuse to give up the faith they have been taught.

for age 9 - 99   **ISBN 0-921100-04-3 Can.\$11.95 U.S.\$9.95**

A Stranger in a Strange Land by **Leonora Scholte**

John E. Marshall in *The Banner of Truth*:This is a delightful book. It tells the story of H.P. Scholte, a preacher in the Netherlands, who being persecuted for his faith in his own country, emigrated to the U.S.A., and there established a settlement in Pella, Iowa, in the midst of the vast undeveloped prairie. . . The greater part of the book is taken up in telling the stories of the immense hardships known after emigration. Interwoven with this story is an account of Scholte's marriage and family life. . . It is a most heartwarming and instructive story.

for age 13-99   **ISBN 0-921100-01-9 Can.$7.95 U.S.$6.90**

A Mighty Fortress in the Storm by **Paulina M. Rustenburg Bootsma**

Fay S. Lapka in *Christian Week*:

[This book] . . . is the fictionalized historical account of the actual village of "Never Thought Of" (literal translation of Nooitgedacht) in the Netherlands, and the efforts of the tiny, two-farm town to aid the resistance. This is a thoroughly interesting, at times warmly-amusing story, that will be enjoyed by adults. The photographs reproduced throughout the text add realism to the amazing story.

for age 13 - 99   **ISBN 0-921100-37-X Can.$11.95 U.S.$10.90**

The Shadow Series by Piet Prins

One of the most exciting series of a master story teller about the German occupation of the Netherlands during the emotional time of the Second World War (1940-1945).

K. Bruning in *Una Sancta* about Vol.4 - *The Partisans*, and Vol. 5 - *Sabotage*: . . . the country was occupied by the German military forces. The nation's freedom was destroyed by the foreign men in power. Violence, persecutions and executions were the order of the day, and the main target of the enemy was the destruction of the christian way of life. In that time the resistance movement of underground fighters became very active. People from all ages and levels joined in and tried to defend the Dutch Christian heritage as much as possible. The above mentioned books show us how older and younger people were involved in that dangerous struggle. It often was a life and death battle. Every page of these books is full of tension. The stories give an accurate and very vivid impression of that difficult and painful time. These books should also be in the hands of our young people. They are excellent instruments to understand the history of their own country and to learn the practical value of their own confession and Reformed way of life. What about as presents on birthdays?

for age 9 - 99

Vol. 1 *The Lonely Sentinel*   ISBN 0-88815-781-9 Can.$7.95 U.S.$6.35
Vol. 2 *Hideout in the Swamp*   ISBN 0-88815-782-7 Can.$7.95 U.S.$6.35
Vol. 3 *The Grim Reaper*   ISBN 0-88815-783-5 Can.$6.95 U.S.$5.65
Vol. 4 *The Partisans*   ISBN 0-921100-07-8 Can.$7.95 U.S.$7.20
Vol. 5 *Sabotage*   ISBN 0-921100-08-6 Can.$7.95 U.S.$7.20

It Began With a Parachute by **William R. Rang**

Fay S. Lapka in *Christian Week*:

[It] . . . is a well-told tale set in Holland near the end of the Second World War. . . The story, although chock-full of details about life in war-inflicted Holland, remains uncluttered, warm and compelling.

for age 8 - 99   **ISBN 0-921100-38-8 Can.$8.95 U.S.$7.90**

Anak, the Eskimo Boy by **Piet Prins**

F. Pronk in *The Messenger*: Anak is an Eskimo Boy, who with his family, lives with the rest of their tribe in the far north. The author describes their day-to-day life as they hunt for seals, caribou and walruses. Anak is being prepared to take up his place as an adult and we learn how he is introduced to the tough way of life needed to survive in the harsh northern climate. We also learn how Anak and his father get into contact with the white man's civilization. . . This book makes fascinating reading, teaching about the ways of Eskimos, but also of the power of the Gospel. Anyone over eight years old will enjoy this book and learn from it.

for age 8 - 99   **ISBN 0-921100-11-6 Can.$6.95 U.S.$6.30**

Tekko and the White Man by Alie Vogelaar

Suddenly a wild thought went through Tekko's mind. If his baby sister didn't recover? Then . . . then . . . he would go to the white medicine man! For a moment he was startled by the thought. Then he was certain of it. They had paid Wemale plenty and offered much to the spirits. If it still didn't help, he would take her to the white medicine man of whom Tani had told him. For a moment he thought about the weird and horrible things Tani also had told him.

for age 7 - 99   **ISBN 0-921100-47-7 Can.$7.95 U.S.$6.90**

Judy's Own Pet Kitten by An Rook

Fay S. Lapka in *Christian Week*: Judy, presumably seven or eight years of age, is the youngest member of a farm family whose rural setting could be anywhere in Canada. The story of Judy, first losing her own kitten, then taming a wild stray cat with kittens, and finally rescuing the tiniest one from a flood, is well-told and compelling.

for age 4 - 10   **ISBN 0-921100-34-5 Can.$4.95 U.S.$4.50**

The Crown of Honour by L. Erkelens

Rachel Manesajian in *Chalcedon Report*: This book is about an illegitimate girl whose mother died when she was born, and no one knows who her father is. She grows up in an orphanage, and she goes through many hardships and is treated poorly because she is illegitimate. The few people she loves are taken away from her. Because of all her trials, she thinks God is against her, and so, in rebellion, she refuses to go to church or pray. However, the prayers of an old man who loves and prays for her are answered and she realizes . . . a wonderful story.

for age 14-99   **ISBN 0-921100-14-0 Can.$11.95 U.S.$10.90**

Living in the Joy of Faith by Clarence Stam
The Christian Faith as Outlined in the Heidelberg Catechism

R.J. Rushdoony in *Chalcedon Report*: In a time of cheap grace, Stam makes clear what the results of redemption are: "Forgiveness is always combined with renewal" (p.178). He makes clear that the term *Holy Gospel* means the Bible, the whole of it, from cover to cover (p.45). It is God communicating with us. "A church that does not preach the Law of God diligently and squarely is an unfaithful church, giving its members false security and withholding from them essential facts, preventing them from leading a life of true happiness in the Lord!" (p.21). On one subject after another, Stam's is the authentic voice of the Reformed faith, speaking with power and with joy. This is a book to prize.

for age 4 - 99   **ISBN 0-921100-27-2 Can.$39.95 U.S.$35.90**

Annotations to the Heidelberg Catechism by J. Van Bruggen

John A. Hawthorne in *Reformed Theological Journal*: . . . The individual Christian would find it a constructive way to employ part of the Sabbath day by working through the lesson that is set for each Lord's Day. No one can study this volume without increasing his knowledge of truth and being made to worship and adore the God of all grace. This book will help every minister in the instruction of his people, both young and not so young, every parent in the task of catechizing and is commended to every Christian for personal study.

                                                 ISBN 0-921100-33-7 Can.$15.95 U.S.$13.90

Proceedings of The International Conference of Reformed Churches
September 1-9, 1993 Zwolle, The Netherlands

Included are the conference papers which were delivered for the general public in the evening sessions.

Section I—Minutes of the Conference
Section II—Speeches and Reports
Section III—Conference Papers

Section IV—Miscellaneous

                                                 ISBN 0-921100-49-3 Can.$9.95 U.S.$8.90

The Belgic Confession and its Biblical Basis by **Lepusculus Vallensis**

The Belgic Confession is a Reformed Confession, dating from the 16th Century, written by Guido de Brès, a preacher in the Reformed Churches of the Netherlands. The great synod of Dort in 1618-19 adopted this Confession as one of the doctrinal standards of the Reformed Churches, to which all office-bearers of the Churches were (and still are) to subscribe. This book provides and explains the Scriptural proof texts for the Belgic Confession by using the marginal notes of the Dutch Staten Bijbel. The Staten Bijbel is a Dutch translation of the Bible, by order of the States General of the United Netherlands, in accordance with a decree of the Synod of Dort. It was first published in 1637 and included 'new explanations of difficult passages and annotations to comparative texts.' **ISBN 0-921100-41-8 Can.$17.95 U.S.$15.90**

Essays in Reformed Doctrine by **J. Faber**

A collection of seventeen articles, speeches, and lectures which are of fundamental importance to all Christians.

Cecil Tuininga in *Christian Renewal*: This book is easy reading as far as the English goes. It can, I judge, be read by all with great profit. . . I found the first chapter on "The Significance of Dogmatology for the Training of the Ministry" excellent. The six essays on the Church I found very informative and worthwhile. . . What makes this book so valuable is that Dr. Faber deals with all the aspects of the Reformed faith from a strictly biblical and confessional viewpoint. **ISBN 0-921100-28-0 Can.$19.95 U.S.$17.90**

The Covenantal Gospel by **C. Van der Waal**

G. Van Rongen in *Una Sancta*: . . . We would like to conclude this review with a quotation from the last lines of this - recommended! - book. They are the following: The Gospel is covenantal in every respect. If things go wrong in the churches, ask whether the covenant is indeed preached and understood.

If missionary work is superficial, ask whether the covenant is taken into account. . . If sects and movements multiply, undoubtedly they speak of the covenant in a strange way, or ignore it deliberately. . . It must be proclaimed. Evangelical = Covenantal. **ISBN 0-921100-19-1 Can.$17.95 U.S.$16.20**

Hal Lindsey and Biblical Prophecy by **C. Van der Waal**

"Hal Lindsey uses Biblical prophecy to open a supermarket," writes the author, "a supermarket in which he sells inside information about the near future, especially World War III. The source of his information are the books of Daniel, Revelation, Ezekiel and Matthew 24. Come, buy and read!"

Dr. Van der Waal not only analyzes Lindsey's weaknesses and mistakes, he also lays down basic guidelines for reading Biblical prophecy - especially the book of Revelation.

ISBN 0-921100-31-0 Can.$9.95 U.S.$8.90

The Relation Between Christian Liberty and Neighbor Love in the Church by **N. D. Kloosterman**

The winding path of this book will lead deep into the evidence of scripture, through the history of Christian ethics, and bring the reader eventually into an open clearing, looking out over the field of Christian ethics itself. Along the way one of the most surprising discoveries will be that what is 'going on' in the offense of the weak involves the relationship between Christian liberty and neighbor love. In fact, these will provide the reader with the points of reference . . .

ISBN 0-921100-30-2 Can.$11.95 U.S.$10.90

Where Everything Points to Him by **K. Deddens**

The Church of Jesus Christ does not live her life in isolation. Even in her corporate worship, she can be adversely influenced by the surrounding culture. Some ministers come to model themselves — even if only unconsciously — after entertainers. And some of the worshipers seem to think that a worship service is essentially a meeting between *people* in which social and aesthetic norms must prevail. In such a climate it is helpful to be reminded of the principles which have shaped corporate worship . . .

ISBN 0-921100-39-6 Can.$12.95 U.S.$11.90

Wholesome Communication by **J.A. Knepper**
A guide to a spiritual conversation.
Pastoral Perspectives I

K.V. Warren in *Vox Reformata*: Here is plenty of practical and down to earth advice as regards the ins and outs of conversation in general: non-verbal communications and its importance, posture, value judgments, leading and structuring a conversation etc.

G. Duncan Lowe in *Covenanter Witness*: This book deserves to be read throughout the Church. It is a manual of practical godliness within a clearly important area, and it is written by a man of experience and sensitivity who continually reflects upon God's Word.

ISBN 0-921100-13-2 Can.$9.95 U.S.$8.90

Christian Philosophy Within Biblical Bounds by **Theodore Plantinga**
In this book, Christian philosophy is described in terms of its relation to such themes and notions as metaphysics, worldview, the limits to knowledge, common grace, Biblical revelation, hermeneutics, and criticism. **ISBN 0-921100-29-9 Can.$7.95 U.S.$6.90**

Church History by **P.K. Keizer**
According to Revelation 12, the history of mankind revolves around the history of Christ's Church.
Hywel Roberts in the *Banner of Truth*:

. . . The author recognizes the true unity of history and relates 'the acts of God's faithfulness and loving-kindness in founding and maintaining the covenant of grace and reconciliation, a covenant that remains valid despite man's disdainful disregard.' **ISBN 0-921100-02-7 Can.$12.95 U.S.$11.90**

Schilder's Struggle for the Unity of the Church by **Rudolf Van Reest**
Klaas Schilder (1890-1952) is remembered both for his courageous stand in opposition to Nazism, which led to his imprisonment three months after the Nazis overran the Netherlands in 1940, and for his role in the Church struggle in the Netherlands, which culminated in 1944 with the suspension of scores of office-bearers and the formation of the liberated Reformed Churches.

Thomas Vanden Heuvel in *The Outlook* of December 1990: I strongly recommend this book for everyone interested in the preservation of and propagation of the Reformed faith.

ISBN 0-921100-23-X Can.$29.95 U.S.$26.60

Seeking Our Brothers in the Light: A Plea for Reformed Ecumenicity
Ed. **Theodore Plantinga**
Al Bezuyen in *Revival*: The book should well serve office bearers and lay people interested in closer contact with the liberated Churches. The work is not exhaustive but rather functions as a spring board from which further study can find a solid beginning and seeks to clear the water that must be entered if ecumenical relations are to take place between the CRC and American / Canadian Reformed Churches.

ISBN 0-921100-48-5 Can.$5.00 U.S.$4.50

About Inheritance Publications

Inheritance Publications is a small company which has been established to provide Biblical Reformed literature. We want to maintain the antithesis between right and wrong, between true and false christianity. It is also our desire to give God the honour and glory due to His Name because of His covenant faithfulness. Remembering the great deeds of God in the history of His Church will always cause God's children to stand in awe for His Majesty. It is our aim to reach children with storybooks about the history of the Church, and adults with books on the doctrine of the Church. May God's Name be glorified and the readers edified by the reading of our books.

WHAT IS THE ADVANTAGE OF BECOMING A MEMBER
OF THE *INHERITANCE BOOK CLUB*?

* As a member you will get the new books of Inheritance Publications at a special price (usually at about 15 % discount) sent to you within about thirty days after publication.

* You have the right to return new I.P. books within 10 days from the day of delivery.

* You don't have to send an order each time a new book is published.

* Members can obtain at any time any number of current I.P. or Premier books at the original special Publication Price, unless the book has been out of print.

* There is no postage charge!

You can join different categories.

Cat. A: Selected new books from Inheritance Publications (about 5 books per year)

Cat. B: Selected new children- and adult-fiction books from I.P. (about 3 books per year)

Cat. C: Selected new study books from I.P. (about 2 books per year)

Cat. D: Selected new books from I.P. and Premier Publishing (about 7 books per year)

Cat. E: Selected new study books from I.P. and Premier Publishing (about 5 books per year)

Inheritance Publications reserves the right to terminate a membership.

Our books are usually based on historical facts or contain sound biblical doctrines.

Titles that are currently available at special prices to I.P. Members:

	reg.price	I.P.member price	
PIET PRINS - SHADOW 4 - THE PARTISANS	CN.$ 7.95	CN.$ 6.75	U.S.$ 5.95
PIET PRINS - SHADOW 5 - SABOTAGE	CN.$ 7.95	CN.$ 6.75	U.S.$ 5.95
PIET PRINS - ANAK, THE ESKIMO BOY	CN.$ 6.95	CN.$ 5.95	U.S.$ 4.95
PIET PRINS - WHEN THE MORNING CAME (STRUGGLE FREEDOM 1)	CN.$ 9.95	CN.$ 8.50	U.S.$ 7.50
J.A. KNEPPER SR. - WHOLESOME COMMUNICATION	CN.$ 9.95	CN.$ 8.50	U.S.$ 7.50
J. FABER - ESSAYS IN REFORMED DOCTRINE	CN.$19.95	CN.$16.95	U.S.$14.95
C. VAN DER WAAL - THE COVENANTAL GOSPEL	CN.$17.95	CN.$15.50	U.S.$13.50
L. ERKELENS - THE CROWN OF HONOUR	CN.$11.95	CN.$ 9.95	U.S.$ 9.25
RUDOLF VAN REEST - SCHILDER'S STRUGGLE FOR UNITY/CHURCH	CN.$29.95	CN.$25.50	U.S.$22.50
P.K. KEIZER - CHURCH HISTORY	CN.$12.95	CN.$10.95	U.S.$ 9.95
T. PLANTINGA - CHRISTIAN PHILOSOPHY WITHIN BIBL. BOUNDS	CN.$ 7.95	CN.$ 6.95	U.S.$ 5.95
N.D. KLOOSTERMAN - THE RELATION BETWEEN CHR. LIBERTY	CN.$11.95	CN.$ 9.95	U.S.$ 9.25
CLARENCE STAM - LIVING IN THE JOY OF FAITH	CN.$39.95	CN.$31.95	U.S.$29.90
J. VAN BRUGGEN - ANNOTATIONS TO THE HEIDELBERG CATECHISM	CN.$15.95	CN.$13.50	U.S.$11.90
C. VANDERWAAL - HAL LINDSEY AND BIBLICAL PROPHECY	CN.$ 9.95	CN.$ 8.50	U.S.$ 7.50
RUDOLF VAN REEST - ISRAEL'S HOPE AND EXPECTATION	CN.$19.95	CN.$16.95	U.S.$14.95
AN ROOK - JUDY'S OWN PET KITTEN	CN.$ 4.95	CN.$ 3.95	U.S.$ 3.60
WILLIAM P. BALKENENDE - LOVE IN TIMES OF REFORMATION	CN.$ 8.95	CN.$ 7.60	U.S.$ 6.60
W.G. VAN DE HULST - WILLIAM OF ORANGE — THE SILENT PRINCE	CN.$ 8.95	CN.$ 7.60	U.S.$ 6.70
HENRY W. CORAY - AGAINST THE WORLD, ATHANASIUS	CN.$ 8.95	CN.$ 7.60	U.S.$ 6.70
WILLIAM R. RANG - IT BEGAN WITH A PARACHUTE	CN.$ 8.95	CN.$ 7.60	U.S.$ 6.70
P.M. RUSTENBURG BOOTSMA - MIGHTY FORTRESS IN THE STORM	CN.$11.95	CN.$10.15	U.S.$ 9.25
K.DEDDENS - WHERE EVERYTHING POINTS TO HIM	CN.$12.95	CN.$10.95	U.S.$10.10
ALIE VOGELAAR - TEKKO AND THE WHITE MAN	CN.$ 7.95	CN.$ 6.75	U.S.$ 5.85
I.C.R.C. - PROCEEDINGS I.C.R.C. 1993	CN.$ 9.95	CN.$ 8.50	U.S.$ 7.50
MARJORIE BOWEN - I WILL MAINTAIN	CN.$17.95	CN.$15.25	U.S.$13.50
LEPUSCULUS VALLENSIS - BELGIC CONFESSION & BIBLICAL BASIS	CN.$17.95	CN.$15.25	U.S.$13.50

INHERITANCE BOOK CLUB MEMBERSHIP FORM

Name _____ Date _____

Address _____

City & Province _____

Postal code _____ Tel. _____

Membership Category _____ Signature _____

Please complete the membership form and return it to:

Inheritance Publications Box 154, Neerlandia, Alberta T0G 1R0 Canada